# A Creative Primary Curricu

The curriculum in many primary schools, in recent history, became worryingly narrowed such that children were being prepared for tests more than their lives were being enriched with a variety of knowledge, skills and experiences. It is clear that it is the latter that enables them to perform well in tests and in life, so the time for change is now! This book seeks to empower teachers and school leaders to better understand what is meant by 'curriculum' and what a creative educational diet might look like in each individual school.

The book explores curriculum intent, implementation and impact. It includes leaders' reflection boxes and practical suggestions for busy teachers. Emma L. Palastanga analyses the need for a broad and balanced curriculum, against the limitations of cramming for success, and delves deep into the process of curriculum planning, delivery and evaluation, using Ofsted's terminology. Examples of lessons and a range of different approaches are shared throughout the book.

*A Creative Primary Curriculum for All* will give all subject leaders, classroom teachers and teacher trainees the confidence to provide a rich, exciting and varied curriculum, meeting the needs of learners whilst also letting the craft of teaching and individual inspiration shine.

**Emma L. Palastanga**, a passionate educator for more than twenty years, has worked in different school settings as a teacher and school leader instigating change. She has also worked as an Ofsted inspector evaluating the quality of education. Emma has experienced different approaches to teaching and learning and felt the pressure of delivering results.

# A Creative Primary Curriculum for All

Emma L. Palastanga

Routledge
Taylor & Francis Group

LONDON AND NEW YORK

First published 2022
by Routledge
2 Park Square, Milton Park, Abingdon, Oxon OX14 4RN

and by Routledge
605 Third Avenue, New York, NY 10158

*Routledge is an imprint of the Taylor & Francis Group, an informa business*

*British Library Cataloguing-in-Publication Data*
*A catalogue record for this book is available from the British Library*

*Library of Congress Cataloging-in-Publication Data*
Names: Palastanga, Emma L., author.
Title: A creative primary curriculum for all / Emma L. Palastanga.
Description: Abingdon, Oxon ; New York, NY : Routledge, 2022. | Includes bibliographical references and index. |
Identifiers: LCCN 2021024228 | ISBN 9780367470715 (hardcover) | ISBN 9780367470722 (paperback) | ISBN 9781003033189 (ebook)
Subjects: LCSH: Education, Primary–Curricula.
Classification: LCC LB1523 .P37 2022 | DDC 372.24/1–dc23
LC record available at https://lccn.loc.gov/2021024228

ISBN: 978-0-367-47071-5 (hbk)
ISBN: 978-0-367-47072-2 (pbk)
ISBN: 978-1-003-03318-9 (ebk)

DOI: 10.4324/9781003033189

Typeset in Bembo Std
by SPi Technologies India Pvt Ltd (Straive)

# Contents

# Acknowledgements

I should like to thank the many people who have supported me in writing this book whether through quiet encouragement, reading the drafts and taking time to provide invaluable feedback or by sharing their own ideas and images and allowing me to freely use them in this text.

Thanks to the publishers who have provided this opportunity, been patient with the delays and answered numerous questions to reassure me.

Thanks to Robert Macfarlane, Granta Publishers and Penguin Random House for granting permission to use an excerpt of 'Mountains of the Mind', an inspiring text in its own right, which also clearly illustrates the need for a creative and cross-curricular approach to a broad and balanced curriculum. Excerpt(s) from MOUNTAINS OF THE MIND: HOW DESOLATE AND FORBIDDING HEIGHTS WERE TRANSFORMED INTO EXPERIENCES OF INDOMITABLE SPIRIT by Robert Macfarlane, copyright © 2003 by Robert Macfarlane.

Used by permission of Pantheon Books, an imprint of the Knopf Doubleday Publishing Group, a division of Penguin Random House LLC. All rights reserved.

Last but by no means least I would like to thank my parents for their support and my wonderful husband, David, for his unfailing belief in me throughout the entire process without whom this book might not have come to fruition!

Thank you to

Bruce, Caroline, Charlie, Colin, David, Louise, Lucy, Lynda, Mary, Martyn, Molly, Penny, Sarah, Spencer, Sushi.

Flickr images are used with thanks to the following:

Kalle Gustafsson for 'Hedgehog II' used in Figure 9.1
Nicolas Raymond for 'Mexico Grunge Flag' used in Figure 9.2
Zwenzini for 'Studying' used in Figure 9.3

# Chapter 1

## Introduction

- What is the aim of this book?
- What classroom experience does the author have?
- How is *curriculum* defined?

The aim of this book is to shine a spotlight on curriculum knowledge, to empower schools to value a broad and balanced curriculum with rich and varied experiences. My experience with and focus in this book are the education system in England; however, there will be similarities with other systems around the world, and much of what I write about will be relevant beyond the UK. Evidence from inspections and wider research evidence in the UK revealed a lack of curriculum knowledge and expertise in schools, which lead to curriculum being confused with assessments, driving the practice of 'teaching to the test' and a narrowed curriculum. Academies have the option of not following the national curriculum, but they must provide a curriculum which is 'broad and balanced' and includes English, maths, science and religious education. I hope this book will inspire educators in a range of settings in terms of both the type of establishment and geographically.

As a passionate educator for twenty years, I have worked in several different school settings from inner city to rural. My roles have encompassed both class teacher and school leader instigating change. I have also worked as an Ofsted inspector, observing and measuring the quality of education in a variety of settings. I have experienced a range of different approaches to teaching and learning as well as feeling the pressure of delivering results. This has led to a narrowed curriculum in Year 6 (the end of primary school in the UK), especially leading up to Statutory Assessments so that time could be spent teaching children how to access tests,

DOI: 10.4324/9781003033189-1

helping children to independently identify how to achieve the full three marks in the reading comprehension paper for example, practising past test papers and providing data analysis to the headteacher termly.

In 2006, I was awarded a master's in education, and as part of this degree, I continued exploring an area which had aroused my curiosity seven years earlier in my Bachelor of Education, namely the 'creative curriculum.' It was elements of this degree which ignited a desire to adopt a more child-centred approach to learning, leading me to take up a post as 'Head of Elementary' in a Montessori school. It was here that I learnt about Dorothy Heathcote's 'Mantle of the Expert' (Heathcote & Bolton 1994) as well as understanding more about the Montessori child-centred approach. On taking up my next post as deputy head in a village primary school, I was tasked with developing the curriculum. This was an exciting and daunting responsibility and something I was determined not to rush. I visited other schools and discussed their learning journeys and carried out literature research to identify our legal obligations and, therefore, our freedoms, after which I led staff meetings to inspire the staff to join me on the voyage.

Teachers need to be given the confidence that providing a rich, exciting and varied curriculum is the right thing to do, and yes, children need to be taught how to access tests but not at the exclusion of all other opportunities. Since 2019, Ofsted has also put a greater emphasis on looking at the curriculum in schools, curriculum intent, implementation and impact, but this has generated a myth for some that there is an 'outstanding curriculum' to be followed. This is simply not true, and there is plenty of scope for the craft of teaching and inspiration to shine through, meeting the needs of learners and impacting on positive outcomes.

For many teachers the word *curriculum* had become synonymous with National Curriculum Programme of Study and Attainment Targets since this is mandatory for all maintained schools in England and Wales, in addition to a daily act of collective worship, religious education and, since September 2020, relationships and sex education (RSE). Relationships education forms part of the mandatory RSE programme which includes online and offline friendships and knowing how to stay safe in the real world and virtual world, as well as respecting and celebrating differences and developing awareness of positive mental wellness in themselves and others. Sex education is compulsory in secondary school but not in primary school; however, some primary schools choose to teach sex education beyond the contents of the science curriculum (which covers how our bodies change as we get older). If a school does decide to teach it, then there should be a separate policy, and parents have a right to withdraw their children from these sessions. It is also imperative to bear in mind religious views and any special educational needs. Relationships education builds the foundation of boundaries and respect, a precursor to consent which is explored at secondary school.

It is the National Curriculum Programmes of Study content which sometimes staff feel pressured to 'get through', and it is this aspect on which the book will **not** focus! The National Curriculum forms one part of the school curriculum, and as stated in the National Curriculum (DfE 2013) document, '[t]he School curriculum comprises all learning and other experiences that each school plans for its pupils'.

The intention of this book is also to empower schools to better understand what is meant by 'curriculum' and 'creativity' and to envisage the educational diet in your school. The curriculum has so much scope for individual creativity and wider opportunities, of which the National Curriculum is only a small part. There are plenty of opportunities for the skill of teaching and individual creativity to shine through, meeting the needs of learners and impacting on positive outcomes. In this vein of empowerment, there will be space to reflect at the end of each chapter with questions to prompt your thinking. Allow yourself some time to absorb what you have read and apply it to your own setting. How would you answer the questions currently, does anything need to change and what other questions or ideas are generated?

In defining *curriculum* we need to explore the purpose of a school curriculum; to do this, I quote from the Education Act 2002 which is cross-referenced in the 2010 Academies Act:

> Every school must offer a curriculum which is balanced and broadly based. Maintained schools must also promote the spiritual, moral, cultural, mental and physical development of pupils at the school and of society and prepare pupils at the school for the opportunities, responsibilities and experiences of later life.
>
> (Parliament of the United Kingdom, 2002 and 2010)

That is to say, schools must provide an education which caters for the current needs of individuals and society as well as prepares children for the future as citizens who have the skill set to contribute to that society. This is where creativity comes into its own; we need citizens who can think creatively, who can solve problems and make connections, who can apply previously learnt knowledge and skills to new situations as jobs and perhaps social situations which don't exist currently but may well exist by the time those children are ready to engage in the world of work. The COVID-19 pandemic has shown us a glimpse of this with many businesses having to adapt, operating in versatile ways and educational establishments having to utilise technology in different ways to continue educating learners beyond the classroom walls.

In Chapter 2, I explore more about the history of the school curriculum so that we can understand the purpose it plays in education today and how this links with creativity as well as where it may have squashed creativity in the past. For now, it is enough to acknowledge from the Education Act 2002 and the Academies Act 2010 quoted earlier that a school curriculum is there for the good of the pupils and of a wider society both at any given moment in time and for the future.

The National Curriculum 'provides pupils with an introduction to the essential knowledge they need to be educated citizens. It introduces pupils to the best that has been thought and said and helps engender an appreciation of human creativity and achievement' (DfE 2013).

If a school follows the National Curriculum, it is a solid foundation for meeting the purpose of a school curriculum; however, note the use of the word *introduction* in the earlier quote, which suggests in itself that there is more to be explored. Later in the 2013 National Curriculum document, this is clarified further: 'The national curriculum is just one element in the education of every child.' Students' education should not be limited to the content of the National Curriculum Programmes of Study. We also need to consider what is meant by 'the best that has been thought and said' as this will differ according to each person's viewpoint. However, the National Curriculum provides some examples from which we can work. This doesn't mean to say that other authors, musicians and artists shouldn't be included. High-quality, well-regarded works should be introduced to children as part of their learning and that, in turn, may stimulate their imagination and model the skills to be learnt in order to produce such pieces. This also applies to mathematical formulae and scientific ideas, in fact, in all areas of the curriculum.

When I was tasked with developing the school curriculum in our small village school, I first began with research. I also explored common myths which existed amongst staff and worked to dispel them. One of the main myths which existed within and beyond my own school was the legal amount of time we must spend teaching core subjects; this does not exist. The Education Act of 2002 states that an order under the act may **not** require allocation of particular periods of time for any programme of study or specific skill or the allocation of particular periods within the school timetable, so yes, you can teach maths in the afternoon if you choose or only teach two sessions of English in a week! This gave us newfound freedoms to block particular subjects so that we taught linked subjects in a particular thematic approach and could spend longer getting deeper into a lesson. This was in contrast to having to stop and change focus every hour, as was previously believed necessary, to fit each subject into a weekly timetable.

In fact, the National Curriculum is a very useful document if you take time to explore it beyond the Programmes of Study because it states quite clearly that schools are also **free to include other subjects or topics** of their choice in **planning and designing their own programme of education**. There is also permission to '**range beyond the national curriculum specifications**' and encouragement for practitioners to '**develop exciting and stimulating lessons** to promote the development of pupils' knowledge, understanding and skills as part of the wider school curriculum' (National Curriculum 2013).

As I stated at the beginning, the term *curriculum* had for many become synonymous with mandatory programmes of study in the National Curriculum. What I hope is now clear is that this is one small part of a child's educational diet during their time at school. I could explore in depth the meaning behind a wide range of terms such as the *taught curriculum*, exactly what it taught and compare that to what the pupils actually learn; the *learned curriculum*; and the *hidden curriculum*, a school's attitudes and culture in general and towards particular subjects, perhaps suggesting through time allocation alone that one subject should be revered more than another or a particular behaviour is more desirable than another. However, for this book, it is enough to simply acknowledge that the National Curriculum Programmes of Study introduce pupils to 'the essential knowledge they need to be educated citizens' (DfE 2013) and that in order to promote the wider development of pupils and prepare them for later life, there are so many more skills, opportunities and experiences we as educators need to provide through exciting and stimulating lessons.

In Chapter 3, I define *creativity* as it is an ambiguous term. By the end of the chapter, you should understand why creativity is important and be able to identify the differences and links between creative teaching, learning and outputs. Creativity is not only of importance to the individual, but it is also imperative for future business and global economic competition.

I draw on the working definition of the *curriculum* that Ofsted has used over the last couple of years in Chapter 5 to explore in more detail the concepts of 'intent,' 'implementation' and 'impact' to 'recognise that the curriculum passes through different states: it is conceived, taught and experienced' (Ofsted 2019).

I dedicate this book to celebrating creative learning opportunities in order to deliver 'exciting and stimulating lessons'. The background information and personal anecdotes are included to support educators on the same journey and to enable you to benefit from my experiences. I hope it will give you the confidence to be brave, take risks and provide your children with high-quality teaching and learning opportunities. Some of the examples included later in the book will link to the national curriculum objectives, and others will explore wider curriculum opportunities.

In the rest of this book, we explore the history of the curriculum, recent changes in the inspection regime and what this has meant for schools whilst providing some examples of creative curriculum lessons as we delve into 'implementation' of curriculum. We also look in more detail about what is meant by a broad and balanced curriculum and the options available to schools. I do not propose one single approach but instead present a range of information which I have gathered in my twenty years in education which I hope will support you to make the right choices for the children in your setting.

---

- What do you understand by 'school curriculum'?
- Did it surprise you to learn that there is no legal time allocation for a subject?
- What does the 'educational diet' look like in your school?
- Is there anything you will adapt or change as a result of reading this chapter?

---

## Bibliography

### Books and articles

Heathcote, D. and Bolton, G. (1994) *Drama for Learning: Dorothy Heathcote's Mantle of the Expert Approach to Education. Dimensions of Drama Series.* Heinemann.

### Journals and reports

DfE (2013) last updated 2015 *The National Curriculum in England: Key Stages 1 and 2 Framework Document* Available from: www.gov.uk/dfe/nationalcurriculum Accessed 3 June 2020.

Ofsted (2019) *Inspecting the Curriculum* Available from: https://www.gov.uk/government/publications/inspecting-the-curriculum Accessed 26 November 2020.

Parliament of the United Kingdom (2002) Education Act 2002 Available from: https://www.legislation.gov.uk/ukpga/2002/32/section/78 3 August 2021.

Parliament of the United Kingdom (2010) *Academies Act 2010* Available from: https://www.legislation.gov.uk/ukpga/2010/32/section/1A Accessed 5 Janurary 2020.

# Chapter 2

## A brief history of the curriculum

- What was the historical purpose of a school curriculum?
- Why was Callaghan's Ruskin speech pivotal?
- How have the goals of education shifted over time?

A school curriculum can be defined as explicitly taught skills, shared knowledge within and across curriculum disciplines and other wider experiences. A school curriculum has been in place for centuries, but what purpose does it serve? Join me on a whistle-stop tour through key points in time to explore the changing educational diet and the rationale behind it.

In ancient Greece around 5 BCE, the formal school curriculum included subjects such as music and dance, which some say served to improve their manoeuvrability as soldiers. The ability to count and record in writing and numbers was necessary for trade. Clarity of speech, as well as the ability to debate, was needed in politics, so these elements also featured in the curriculum as pupils developed their basic skills and progressed further in their education. It is clear to see how the curriculum taught at school related directly to the skills these Greek citizens would require in later life. Let us now speed forward to the more modern Victorian era to explore the influences at play.

In Victorian England (1837–1901), class and gender impacted the curriculum. Wealthy families sent their children to fee-paying schools where boys were taught to be gentlemen so that they could become members of the elite class; their curriculum consisted of sportsmanship, religion, leadership and confidence, whereas girls were taught sewing, cooking, drawing and music, skills that would benefit them

DOI: 10.4324/9781003033189-2

when they got married. In fact, the purpose of girls learning these skills was so that they would be able help their future husband and make him proud according to some texts on the subject! Poor children would often be working and providing an income to their families; factory work and mining were particularly common. The Elementary Education Act of 1870 was the first of a number of acts of parliament passed between 1870 and 1893 to create compulsory education in England and Wales for children aged between 5 and 13. It brought into force changes such as public funding for schools, non-denominational religious education, which parents had a right to withdraw their children from, and school inspections to maintain standards of education. A basic curriculum was delivered so that they could read (especially the Bible for a good moral grounding), and some skills such as gardening and knitting were taught to ensure children had the skills as adults to maintain a home and earn a living. In summary, skills taught at school prepared the children for life in the future as responsible citizens and was tailored to their projected future path. We hasten onwards now to a time in living memory for many into the 1970s.

A speech, 'A Rational Debate Based on the Facts' given by Labour Prime Minister James Callaghan in Ruskin College Oxford on 18 October 1976, is widely regarded as having begun the 'Great Debate' about the nature and purpose of public education. Callaghan highlighted that for years, the focus of education was to provide enough learning to ensure the future workforce could earn their living in a factory, and he was keen to stress that there was more to education than just preparing workers to oil the wheels of the economy.

In his speech, Callaghan (1976) argued for a balance of skills for work and attitudes for life. He said that there is little benefit to producing 'socially well-adjusted members of society' who are lacking skills and are therefore unemployed but counterbalances this argument by saying that we are not aiming to produce 'technically efficient robots' at the other end of the scale. He highlighted that both purposes require the same tools:

[B]asic literacy, basic numeracy, the understanding of how to live and work together, respect for others, respect for the individual. This means requiring certain basic knowledge, and skills and reasoning ability. It means developing lively inquiring minds and an appetite for further knowledge that will last a lifetime. It means mitigating as far as possible the disadvantages that may be suffered through poor home conditions or physical or mental handicap.

(Callaghan 1976 cited by Gillard 2018a)

These are the same aims we have for education today, although our appreciation of 'disadvantage' is much broader, and we also include vulnerable groups of children through ethnicity, gender and socio-economic background. For some of those who are disadvantaged, we now have the pupil-premium grant in place so that schools can target the needs of children who have been eligible for free school meals in the last six years or are currently eligible, those who are looked after through adoption, those who have a special guardianship order or those with a child arrangement order. Also, to support pupils' pastoral needs for those with parents in the services, there is the 'Service Premium'. These funds are in place to help schools mitigate disadvantage as much as possible. Elements of this approach can be seen in Victorian times, although it depended on the path you were likely to take; being a lady or a gentleman was quite different from keeping a tidy home or doing factory work. Now Callaghan proposed a new approach:

> The goals of our education, from nursery school through to adult education, are clear enough. They are to equip children to the best of their ability for a lively, constructive, place in society; and also to fit them to do a job of work. Not one or the other but both.
>
> (Callaghan 1976 cited by Gillard 2018a)

Having established the core purpose of the national curriculum, we now need to dive a little deeper into the detail within a more recent historical period. The first statutory national curriculum was introduced by the Education Reform Act 1988 by Kenneth Baker; this was an incredibly detailed and prescriptive curriculum with little room for teacher creativity and limited space for any additional learning opportunities. This helps us understand why there has been some confusion from teachers and school leaders over the freedoms now afforded them and the confusion between the school curriculum and the national curriculum. Since this initial introduction, there have been periodic reviews, starting with Ron Dearing in 1993, which slimmed down some of the content and complexity of the previous document. A further slimming of the curriculum took place in 1998, disapplying the statutory Programmes of Study for the foundations subjects so that more time could be spent teaching literacy and numeracy, which was also the focus of a new national curriculum introduced in 1999, reducing content in foundation subjects so that more time could be spent on English, maths and science. Whilst a 'broad and balanced curriculum' was still being advocated, conversely, there was the introduction of national strategies such as 'The Literacy Hour' and 'The Numeracy

Hour' to drive up standards in these core curriculum areas alongside the reduction of content in foundation subjects. It is understandable to see where the concept of a narrowed curriculum may have been further compounded. In 2009, Jim Rose conducted his review of the curriculum with proposals to group subjects under 'areas of learning' and to further slim the curriculum, however, plans for this curriculum were abandoned after a change in government in 2010. In 2013, Tim Oates led a review which contributed to the new curriculum in 2013/14. This newest curriculum, whilst being clear and directive, also allowed some greater space for teacher creativity and flexibility, although it would take some time before this was fully recognised within the profession. It is hardly surprising when you consider the number of changes over time and note how detailed the first national curriculum was. Many of the school leaders of today would have been teaching from the 1988 curriculum in their early days, and whilst all educational professionals keep themselves up-to-date, some implicit historical messages may be hard to ignore.

In summary, we can see that since the times of ancient Greece, the core purpose of education has been to prepare citizens for their future lives as adults in society. This includes the skills required not only to work and earn a living but also to contribute to society more widely, to engage with others respectfully and to understand ourselves as individuals. For me personally, this is one of the magical moments in teaching; seeing young people mature and solve their own conflicts peacefully, once they have the tools and practice to do so confidently and to understand social conventions and apply them in context. I will always remember a child with complex and challenging behavioural needs passing the bread rolls to another at a Year 6 leavers' dinner and engaging in polite conversation. I like to think that our input as teachers supporting the choices children make as well as modelling good behaviour helps children prepare for their future as much as teaching them the skills of reading, writing and maths! Whilst the core purpose of education has not changed in centuries, what is required of adults in society changes constantly, and so our curricula must reflect that. Sir Ken Robinson (2010) says that the world is changing faster now than ever before and that '[o]ur best hope for the future is to develop a new paradigm of human capacity to meet a new era of human existence' he suggests that ' [w]e need to create environments ... where every person is inspired to grow creatively'. I couldn't agree more, and this is the reason that a creative curriculum is so important: enabling learners to make connections, solve problems and share their creative outputs and providing them with the tools to adapt to new situations by utilising skills and knowledge they have learned in different contexts so that our future citizens are able to create solutions to problems.

In recent years, there has been a greater focus on technology both in the workplace and in the classroom; without it, educating in the lockdowns of 2020 due to the COVID-19 pandemic would have been a greater challenge than it was, with a large number of students being able to access a digital device connected to the internet. It was through students' developed competency and the rapid 'upskilling' of staff which enabled a situation close to normality for those children. Mental health is also a key area for education if we are to support children to develop as rounded and healthy citizens for the future. A well-rounded education should incorporate good self-care, and if we support this in primary school and throughout a child's education, we will be enhancing and potentially saving lives (now or in the future) of those children who wouldn't otherwise be aware of a range of support and strategies. Introducing them to these resources early will educate them to understand the need for a balanced lifestyle to nurture a sense of well-being. In addition to this, we will be reducing the impact on the National Health Service in the future years of individuals who may otherwise have needed ongoing mental health support once they have reached a crisis point or long-term mental health issues. The COVID-19 pandemic has sharply focused our minds on this since it will have affected so many people in so many different ways and schools are encouraged to support learners with their well-being. I hope that this is something which becomes embedded for the long term. If we equip children with the tools to talk about their own mental health and that of others and to know where to go for support, education could end the stigma of mental health and signpost early help for those who need it.

Being made aware of the history of a curriculum was a turning point for me, it was the point at which I began to question my pedagogy. Rather than being a robotic teacher, I began to analyse and evaluate what I was teaching and why. In the next chapter, we explore the new terminology in use by Ofsted which examines our practice further. Before you move on, allow yourself some time for reflection using the prompts in the reflection box.

---

**What is your intent for the school curriculum?**

- Why are we teaching this skill?
- Why is this piece of knowledge needed, and how is it built on?
- How will this serve our future society?

---

## Biblography

Books and articles

Dearing, R. (1993) *The National Curriculum and Its Assessment Final Report* London: School Curriculum and Assessment Authority.

DfE (1999) *The National Curriculum in England: Handbook for primary teachers in England* Available from: https://dera.ioe.ac.uk/18150/7/QCA-99-457_Redacted.pdf Accessed 3 June 2020.

Gillard, D. (2018a) *Jim Callaghan - Ruskin College speech (1976) Education in England: A history* Available from: http://www.educationengland.org.uk/documents/ speeches/1976ruskin.html Accessed 6 July 2020.

Gillard, D. (2018b) *Education Reform Act (1988) Education in England: A history* Available from: http://www.educationengland.org.uk/documents/acts/1988-education-reform-act.pdf Accessed 6 July 2020.

Robinson, K. (2010) *The Element: How Finding Your Passion Changes Everything* London: Penguin.

Rose, J. (2009) *Independent Review of the Primary Curriculum: Final Report* Nottingham: DCSF Publications Available from: http://www.educationengland.org.uk/ documents/pdfs/2009-IRPC-final-report.pdf Accessed 17 March 2020.

Rose, J. (2010) *Rose Review officially abandoned* Available from: https://resource-bank. scholastic.co.uk/content/Rose-Review-officially-abandoned-11405 Accessed 6 July 2020.

Journals and reports

Parliament House of Lords (1870) *The 1870 Education Act* Available from: https:// www.parliament.uk/about/living-heritage/transformingsociety/livinglearning/ school/overview/1870educationact/ Accessed 8 July 2020.

Websites

Oates, T. (2013) *Opening the door to deeper understanding* Available from: https://www. cambridgeassessment.org.uk/insights/national-curriculum-tim-oates-on-assess-ment-insights/ Accessed 17 March 2020.

# Chapter 3

## Constraints, creativity, carte blanche?

- What are the legal constraints of a mainstream primary school, and how does this differ for an academy?
- What is creativity, and how does this apply to teachers as well as the young minds we aim to inspire?
- Why do we need a national curriculum at all? Pre-1988, schools, guided by exam syllabus and employers' requirements, could decide what to teach; should we bring this approach back?

Now we have defined *curriculum* and understanding more about its history, this chapter focuses on the constraints felt by teachers and how much freedom there is in terms of creativity as well as whether a carte blanche approach is the way forward.

A constraint is defined as a limitation or restriction, and many teachers have felt this way for too long. It is a legacy of the prescriptive 1988 national curriculum which left little room for teacher input, and the Qualifications and Curriculums Authority offered guidance on time allocations for each subject which many schools assumed as 'law' rather than guidance. When I first introduced the changes to the school curriculum, in the small village school, we examined what was mandatory and the freedoms we had. It was a common misconception amongst the group of staff I was working with that specific subjects must have specific time allocations, as I mentioned in Chapter 1, and this was also true for a wider audience. This had stemmed, in part, from guidance documents which made suggested time allocations, and these had then been wrongly understood to be mandatory. This was a revelation to many and immediately removed the metaphorical shackles which felt

DOI: 10.4324/9781003033189-3

very rigid but were, in fact, found to not even exist! Whilst in the past the National Curriculum and Early Years Foundation Stage Framework may have been restrictive, as Amanda Spielman (2019), HM chief inspector of education, children's services and skills, eloquently puts it, these documents are there to 'carry the load'. They set out the basics all children should be taught and experience. Whilst academies, free schools and independent schools are not duty-bound to follow the National Curriculum, many, in fact, do use it as a basis or may select from a range of other approaches, which I will delve into in Chapter 8.

This freedom comes with responsibility and a keen desire to move away from a tick-box mentality. Criticism of a tick box mentality is highlighted in the Ofsted (2009) document *Improving Primary Teachers' Subject Knowledge across the Curriculum*: 'The teaching was directed towards a predetermined outcome, set out in the scheme of work. Many of the teachers did not know how to promote pupils' creativity, either by leaving the initiative with the pupil or by intervening'. This statement is made in relation to weaker teaching in art. However, pause and reflect; this could be true of any subject. Is creativity encouraged in maths, English, science or music for example by either intervening or leaving the initiative to the pupil, or is creativity limited by directing learners towards a predetermined outcome? It was for this reason that the school I led this development in were encouraged to plan its own curriculum and not use something 'off the shelf'. We discussed with the children topics that excite and engage them, and from this, we selected a topic area that would draw together several areas of the curriculum, enabling us to make links as we naturally do in the real world and provide a meaningful context like a metaphorical coat hanger from which the chosen areas of the curriculum would 'hang'.

Having defined *curriculum* in Chapter 1, it is now important to explore what is meant by 'creativity'. In 2015, the Rt Hon Nick Gibb MP explained that '[e]ducation is the engine of our economy, it is the foundation of our culture, and it's an essential preparation for adult life'. (DfE & Gibb 2015) He also says it is about 'ensuring that young people receive the preparation they need to secure a good job and a fulfilling career and have the resilience and moral character to overcome challenges and succeed'. This is not too dissimilar to a statement from the Department for Education and Employment twenty years earlier stating that the government's principal aim for education is '[t]o support economic growth and improve the Nation's competitiveness and quality of life … by promoting an efficient and flexible labour market' (DfEE 1995, 1). We need creative thinkers in our society in order to benefit individuals in connecting with their sense of identity and to encounter fulfilment as stated by Ken Robinson (2010) or, as Csikszentmihalyi (2008) puts it, to experience 'flow'. We also need creative thinkers for the future economy and global competition; we need a workforce that continues to be innovative and has the capacity to solve future problems that currently do not exist. This has been only too evident during the COVID-19 pandemic, with businesses having to adapt and change in order to survive and many individuals having to explore alternative options as their industries were temporarily or permanently closed.

There are implications for the teacher's role in developing this facet in the classroom. Very few teachers are unfamiliar with the term *creativity*; however, it is questionable as to whether each teacher shares the same definition as policymakers and researchers. The National Advisory Committee on Creative and Cultural Education (NACCCE) report (1999) stated that a survey of teachers and lecturers found that many people associated creativity primarily with 'the arts', and it is my feeling that so long as there is a cross-curricular link to drama, music, dance and art, teachers and curriculum policymakers will feel that they are meeting the needs identified by educational research. My understanding of creative thinking goes deeper than this; it is applicable to and desirable in all subjects and an intrinsic part of the learning process.

*Creativity* is an extremely broad term, which can lead to ambiguity amongst practitioners. It can be defined in terms of creative learning, teaching and creative output. These are all interlinked; creative teaching should foster creative thinking, which may or may not lead to visible 'outputs'. These 'outputs' could be a strategy or an approach to solving a problem rather than an artistic 'piece'. I shall focus less on the output and more on teaching and, first, learning. Children need to develop skills which Anna Craft (2000) defines as 'little creativity' to describe the 'kind of creativity which guides choices and route-finding in everyday life' (p. 3). I will adopt the terms *intellectual creativity* or *creative thinking* throughout to be synonymous with *little creativity*. Fryer (1996) argued that 'to cope with the demands of the future, people will have to be quick-thinking, flexible and imaginative … they will need to be competent in producing effective solutions to unfamiliar problems in unclear situations' (p. 5). This is in line with both Craft's and my own understanding of intellectual creativity. Fryer also said that most of what children are learning in school will no longer be applicable to them as adults in the workplace due to the 'explosion' of new knowledge. We need to have a workforce that continues to be innovative and sufficiently adaptable to cope with future demands posed by a global economy and international competition placing intellectual creativity at the forefront of a modern curriculum fit for the future. Fryer (1996) highlights the investment that large organizations have made in training staff to become skilled in creative problem-solving; this has enabled them to remain market leaders and to be financially viable in the face of competition. Education, historically, has laid the foundations for a skilled workforce; however, traditional 'factory' schooling, as both Egan (1992, as cited by Fryer) and Glasser (1992, as cited in Fryer) have argued, is no longer appropriate to the needs of modern organizations (cited in Fryer 1996). The concept of a 'job for life' is no longer the norm and therefore it is in the interests of the individual to have a flexible approach. Storr (1988, cited in Fryer 1996) has pointed out that creative skills enable us to be flexible enough to adapt and change.

Creative teaching therefore needs to develop the skills which children require. In Hong Kong, Singapore and the Republic of Korea, 'creative thinking' is viewed as the basis for all learning (Hastings 2004). Clarke (2003) highlights the need for creative thinkers by stating that in addition to teaching children skills and knowledge, education at primary school should also be about problem-solving and the joy of experiencing discovery for themselves. I would agree with Bloom (cited in Fryer 1996), who has argued that schooling often (especially historically) neglected higher-order thinking processes, which was detrimental to many children's long-term education and prospects; however, with the introduction of the new maths mastery curriculum for example, we are seeing a change with the inclusion of reasoning and problem-solving being core components of the curriculum. My experience has shown that those students who are enabled to think creatively have been more engaged in the learning process and developed greater self-esteem as a direct result of making a positive contribution. Having established that there is a need for creative thinkers and that education plays a vital role in developing this ability, how this can best be achieved is next discussed.

Creative thinking cannot occur in a vacuum but requires knowledge to underpin it and a conducive environment in which to explore new avenues of thought. A certain degree of confidence is required in order to question existing ideas and facts, and it is the teacher's responsibility to nurture this. The NACCCE (1999) report supported the view that creative education should be promoted in all areas of the curriculum and not exclusively through the 'creative subjects'. This is also my view. Dearden (1968), cited by Foster (1971), suggested a complex role for teachers, including questioning, hinting, inviting contradictions, feigning ignorance, posing problems and pretending perplexity to stimulate critical learning. I would agree that this is indeed a complex role, particularly if we also take into consideration all the other requirements of teachers to impart knowledge and develop skills, as well as their pastoral responsibilities. Nonetheless, developing creative thinkers is an integral part of teaching and learning, and therefore, this role is not only complex but also crucial. Some research suggests that 'discovery methods' are important and that home and school should give 'free reign' to the child; perhaps *progressive teaching* would be an applicable term to use; however, there are many contradictory views that suggest independence, imagination and curiosity are important for creative thinking but so, too, is some structure and guidance or 'formal instruction'. It would be interesting for example to see how well a child learnt to read through play and exploration rather than through instruction. Foster (1971) places the importance on the role of the teacher: 'The interaction of the teacher with the well-timed, carefully posed question does guide the thinking and is a great spur to further original thought' (p. 151).

Foster (ibid) also maintains that

[m]uch potential is only realised if the teacher is able to recognise creative behaviour and … encourage it. This will probably best be accomplished … where the individual is respected and genuine participation is encouraged, the teacher joining in and carefully guiding the pupil's thinking.

(p. 157)

This quote implies the importance of 'guidance' in developing creative thinkers and not giving complete free rein to children; it is essential that this point is understood by practitioners when promoting 'creativity' in practice. Sidney Parnes, co-founder of the Creative Education Foundation, goes so far as to suggest that the *facilitators* of creativity need to demonstrate that they can work well as a group; show sincere enthusiasm, optimism and spontaneity; and be open to ideas and ready to take calcu-lated cognitive risks. Parnes supports the view that teachers are directly involved in affecting the extent of creative thinking that children can engage in. Torrance and Myers (1970, cited in Fryer 1996) support a structured approach and an important role for the teacher because they state that teaching creatively demands dedication and sensitivity, plus a need to recognise and encourage further effort. It is clear that a laissez-faire approach is not promoted in the research literature and that the nature of the teacher's views and their approach can directly affect the opportunities presented to children in order to develop their creative thinking. I do not explore a detailed assessment of creative traits as I am more interested in the creative *process* than *outcomes*. Because of the scope of this, I have also limited my work primarily to the British education system and policies whilst being mindful of the need to consider the implications of globalisation.

Developing creative thinking has huge implications for teaching and learning, not least of which is understanding its nature. Torrance (1965 as cited in Foster 1971) defines creative thinking as sensing a problem, void, or anomaly, guessing and hypothesising about it, evaluating and testing ideas, possibly re-evaluating and retesting and communicating results. In addition to these aspects, creative thinkers recognise analogies between one area and another. It has also been suggested that mature, highly creative people think for themselves and seek to not only open their own minds but those of others as well. They can display a tendency to spend long periods trying to integrate and evaluate their own thinking with that of others (MacKinnon 1962, 1978, Barron 1969, ibid). So we can see here that group work, thematic learning, making links between subject knowledge and skills and communicating learning to each other are nurturing environments for creative thinking.

Fifty-three years ago, in 1967, Plowden suggested that it was important to develop a child's personality and satisfy curiosity (as cited in Marsh 1997). This is as relevant today as it was then. Curiosity is noted by many to be an important starting point for creative thinking: the need to know why or how, in effect, identifying a problem that requires a solution. Many young children are naturally curious, and in order to maintain a degree of curiosity, it is important to allow children time to play and explore for themselves before intervening. In my own science teaching, for example, I often allow children to explore the equipment for themselves (having given safety instructions!) before asking them what they have found out and exploring together why this is so. Imagination is crucial to continuing the creative thinking process, a problem could be identified but left without a solution. Fryer (1996) believes that '[t]o encourage their creativity, students should be given plenty of opportunities to imagine in the sense of thinking for themselves' (p. 51). Imagination allows the thinker to explore possibilities, and Storr (1988) sees imagination as 'biologically adaptive' because it allows us to compare our current situation with what is possible (Fryer 1996). Imaginative thought may lead to many possible solutions, and this can be termed 'divergent thinking'. A truly creative thinker demonstrates the interdependence of convergent (collecting lots of ideas and distilling them into one) and divergent thinking (starting from one idea and generating many possibilities). Craft (2000) argues that possibility thinking, as she terms it, is the basis of creativity and is involved in convergent and divergent thinking. Some may argue that creativity is completely separate from intellect, but I would agree with Guilford (cited in Foster 1971) in that a total picture of intelligence includes a variety of creative abilities.

In summary, I have identified the term *intellectual creativity* to define the thinking process as coming up with new ideas and solutions to problems. I have also established the need for creative thinkers in terms of a global economy to meet changing economic requirements. Historically, education has been a part of the process of preparing a skilled workforce. The requirements of a 'skilled workforce' have changed and the development of a school curriculum has not always kept pace with these needs. Creativity in the classroom is more than just a time for children to play, which is how I consider that some may have supposed or to achieve a creative output in the arts for example. Curiosity and imagination play a large part in fostering creative thought, and as teachers, it is our responsibility to provide opportunities for play and to use questioning techniques to draw out children's ideas that may otherwise remain hidden. Intellect is multifaceted, and like Perkins (1981), I maintain that if education is failing to stimulate creative thinking, then we are neglecting one of the most crucial skills required for our future. Perkins regards creativity as 'the mind's best work' (1981 p. 274, as cited by Fryer 1996). Fryer suggests that Perkins implies a belief that the delivery of the curriculum must address all aspects of creative development. She suggests that if this is achieved, providing a good education and developing creativity will be regarded as tantamount (Fryer 1996). I concur with the need to develop creative thinking within a broad and balanced curriculum. I have merely scratched the surface of creative thinking and the implications for teaching. There is much scope for further research; however, I hope I have highlighted the need to provide children with open-ended challenges to apply their knowledge across the curriculum and beyond it to new situations. The teacher's role is crucial in the timely use of questions to develop thinking further, inviting contradictions and encouraging children to make links between their own thinking and that of others. In addition feigning ignorance and encouraging children to find solutions to problems scaffolds their creative thinking. This approach would develop a skill for life which will benefit the individual as much as the economy.

It should now be very clear that the National Curriculum and Early Years Foundation Stage Framework are useful documents which set out the basics and that a creative approach to education is necessary to ensure a globally competitive workforce. The National Curriculum and Early Years Foundation Stage Framework are only a small part of the school curriculum, and wider experiences within a broad and balanced curriculum provide enjoyment and excitement. Teachers have a number of freedoms to enrich the curriculum. I share a few examples in Chapter 7 which I hope will inspire you further. A curriculum should be as unique as the school it is taught in, but what is it that makes a school unique? There are many answers to this question including the geographical location and the history of the school including perhaps its alumni, its current cohort of children and staff and the building itself. This is all before we begin to look at the lifeblood of the school: the children and staff who each bring their own unique experiences and beliefs with them. If a school is near a coast, then it is likely that children will enjoy a greater awareness of their local beaches and oceans even before they start school and that this natural resource will be tapped into for a range of learning opportunities which is in stark contrast to children attending an inner-city school for example, with limited open spaces yet fascinating architecture and, in some cases, a more multi-cultural community which brings with it a wealth of learning opportunities denied to those schools with a more homogeneous cohort. One school I am familiar with takes their children ice-skating, which encourages children, particularly those from disadvantaged backgrounds, to engage in the wider curriculum. Another has several Muslim parents, so when teaching about Islam in religious education, these parents are invited in to share their own experiences and talk about their beliefs. One primary academy with a large number of deaf pupils has chosen to teach British sign language to all students, which enables everyone to communicate with each other and fosters inclusion in a very practical sense.

Is carte blanche the way forward? Carte blanche literally translates as blank paper. If we look back at the 1944 Education Act, which stated that each education authority should 'contribute towards the spiritual, moral, mental and physical development of the community', the only stipulation was that all schools must teach religious education. It pretty much embodies 'carte blanche'. The curriculum in primary and, indeed, early secondary education was determined for the most part by the teachers and available textbooks, and for older children, it was based on an exam syllabus. The purpose of a national curriculum is to set out a minimum educational expectation for every child. It is useful to start from a basic national minimum to ensure a degree of uniformity in basic skills which there may not be if every individual school is left to decide for itself in the carte blanche approach. It is all about balance: a balance of uniform skills and minimum requirements with the creative freedom to design a unique curriculum which meets the needs of the pupils within the establishment.

---

- What do you understand *creativity* to mean, and has your view changed?
- How do you already develop creativity, and is there anything you would change?
- Do you see the Early Years Framework and National Curriculum as a constraint or a springboard?

---

## Bibliography

Books and articles

Barron, F. (1969) *Creative person and creative process*, New York: Holt; Rinehart, & Winston.

Craft, A. (2000) *Creativity across the primary curriculum; framing and developing practice*, London: Routledge.

Csikszentmihalyi, M. (2008) *Flow: The psychology of optimal experience*, New York: Harper Perennial.

Dearden, R.F. (1968) *The philosophy of primary education*, London: Routledge.

DfEE (1995) *The english education system: An overview of structure and policy*, London: DfEE.

DfE & Gibb, N. (2015) *Speech: The purpose of education*, London: DfE Available from: https://www.gov.uk/government/speeches/the-purpose-of-education Accessed 19 February 2020.

Foster, J. (1971) *Creativity and the teacher*, London: Macmillan Education Ltd.

Fryer, M. (1996) *Creative teaching and learning*, London: Paul Chapman Publishing Ltd.

MacKinnon, D.W. (1978) *In search of human effectiveness*, Buffalo, NY: Bearly.

Marsh, C.J. (1997) *Planning management and ideology; key concepts for understanding the curriculum*, London: The Falmer Press.

NACCCE (1999) *All our futures: Creativity culture and education*, Suffolk: DfEE.

Perkins, D.N. (1981) *The mind's best work*, Cambridge, MA: Harvard University Press.

Robinson, K. & Arnica, L. (2010) *The element: How finding your passion changes everything*, USA: Viking Penguin.

## Journals and reports

Clarke, C. (2003) *Excellence and Enjoyment - A Strategy for Primary Schools*. Available from: https://dera.ioe.ac.uk/4817/7/pri_excel_enjoy_strat_Redacted.pdf Accessed 8 April 2020.

Gillard, D. (2018) *The Curriculum from 5 to 16 HMI Series: Curriculum Matters No. 2 (1985)* London: Her Majesty's Stationery Office. Available from: http://www.educationengland.org.uk/documents/hmicurricmatters/curriculum.html Accessed 5 June 2020.

Glasser, W. (1992) The quality school curriculum. *Phi Delta Kappan, 73* (9), 690–694.

Hastings, S. (2004) *Creativity* TES February 27, 11–14.

MacKinnon, D.W. (1962) The nature and nurture of creative talent. *American Psychologist, 17*(7), 484–495.

Ofsted (2009) *Improving primary teachers' subject knowledge across the curriculum*, London: Ofsted. Available from: https://dera.ioe.ac.uk/305/1/Improving%20primary%20teachers%20subject%20knowledge%20across%20the%20curriculum.pdf Accessed 12 May 2020.

Spielman, A. (2019) *Education inspection framework 2019: Inspecting the substance of education – Foreword*, London: Osfted. Available from: https://www.gov.uk/government/consultations/education-inspection-framework-2019-inspecting-the-substance-of-education/education-inspection-framework-2019-inspecting-the-substance-of-education Accessed 10 March 2020.

# Chapter 4

## A broad and balanced curriculum

- What might a 'broad and balanced' curriculum look like?
- Why is cramming for success prevalent and futile?
- How has the Ofsted framework changed, and did it previously have an impact on narrowing the curriculum?

So far, we have developed a deeper understanding of the term *curriculum*, we have an overview of some points in history to illustrate how 'curriculum' is determined by the society and times we live in and we have explored and reflected on what this might mean for us in the here and now. In this chapter, I analyse the terms *broad* and *balanced*. These terms are intertwined when describing the needs of a curriculum; however, I pull them apart to define them more clearly in this chapter.

A broad curriculum is one with a wide range and variety of subjects taught and experiences built in. It is vitally important to give learners a breadth of knowledge and skills to prepare them for later life as, unlike the Victorian era, we do not predict what their future path might be and teach according to this. Instead, we need to provide young people with a multitude of skills and information so that they can make their own choices later in life about which path they may choose to follow. Both Nick Gibb (DfE & Gibb 2015) in his speech on the purpose of education and James Callaghan (1976) in his Ruskin College speech (cited by Gillard 2018), commonly referred to as 'The Great Debate in Education', are clear that there must be a balance of purpose in learning for the child themselves and as a citizen who should have the skills to support the economy. Gibb stated that we should be

DOI: 10.4324/9781003033189-4

'instilling in them a love of knowledge and culture for their own sake … ensuring (they) receive the preparation they need to secure a good job … and have the resilience and moral character to overcome challenges and succeed.'

Each subject has an important place in the curriculum and in the skills set which enables and enhances understanding of other curriculum areas. We will now look at each subject in turn from its starting point in the Early Years through to the National Curriculum until the end of Key Stage 2 to analyse this in more detail.

## English

The Early Years building blocks for English gives children opportunities to listen to and understand each other and adults as well as to converse in a variety of group sizes and settings. Speaking and listening is a crucial skill for getting by in life as well as the basis for learning across the curriculum. Encouraging children to link sounds (phonemes) and letters (graphemes) enables them to begin to decode, comprehend, read and write. In later years, the focus is fluency so that they communicate their ideas and emotions to others efficiently and effectively through speaking and writing. With the development of reading and listening, they are able to engage with what others are communicating. Reading and drama also offer the opportunity to develop culturally, emotionally, intellectually, socially and spiritually.

## Mathematics

Mathematics is needed in our daily life; it is vital to science, technology and engineering as well as most other jobs. Mathematics provides a foundation for understanding the world. Foundation skills provide children with opportunities to develop skills in counting concrete objects as well as understanding and using numbers and identifying patterns, and once these are secure, they can apply these skills to calculating simple addition and subtraction problems. As pupils gain confidence and deepen their understanding, they are encouraged to manipulate numbers, explain their thinking and look for alternative solutions to problems. Problem-solving and reasoning are critical elements of creative thinking; justifying your thinking in maths is a skill which can be used across the curriculum to justify viewpoints.

## Science

Children enjoy finding things out for themselves and in fact, this is one of the 'Characteristics of Effective Learning' in the Early Years. Science provides many opportunities for exploration and for children to work cooperatively in solving problems. In the Early Years, 'Exploring the World' provides opportunities for children to explore, observe and find out more about the natural world and to understand important changes that we can observe. Science teaching and learning help develop an understanding and respect of the environment. It encourages systematic working, reasoning and develops skills such as questioning, observation, measuring and recording and identifying patterns and relationships.

## Art and design

Expressive arts and design at the start of children's time in school involve enabling children to explore and play with a wide range of media and materials, as well as providing opportunities for sharing their thoughts, ideas and feelings through a variety of activities in the expressive arts. Art equips children with the knowledge and skills to experiment, invent and create their own works of art, crafts and design; it is creative thinking expressed through creative output. Art can support critical thinking; learning how art and design have been influenced by history and continue to reflect culture.

## Design technology

In design technology, pupils use cross-curricular subject knowledge and skills and apply these to new situations; in other words, they think creatively to solve practical problems. They learn how to take risks, solve problems, adapt and question past and present designs and technologies and understanding their impact on our lives.

## Computing

In the Early Years, many practitioners provide opportunities for learners to use programmable toys to support their learning, building a basis for coding later in life. Computing requires the application of creative thinking to solve problems, especially in programming. Computing is strongly linked with maths, science and technology and has many transferable skills as well as applications for other subject areas. Despite the fast-paced change of technology, the skills taught in computing enables pupils to be confident and creative users of technology and information, as well as being able to express themselves and develop their ideas so that they can become active participants in the world. Through understanding and applying the fundamentals of computer science, they should also be able to write appropriate computer programs in order to solve problems.

## Geography

In the Early Years, 'Understanding the World' involves guiding children to make sense of their physical world and their community through opportunities to explore, observe and find out about people, places and the environment. Geography continues to inspire a curiosity and fascination about the world. It equips pupils with knowledge about diverse environments, people, and resources. Creative thinking is required to make links between the differences and to understand experiences beyond our own.

## History

'Understanding the World' in the Early Years sets the basis for children under-standing the past and present educating about Britain's past and that of the wider world. It encourages pupils to be curious about the past understanding how people and places change and to foster critical thinking, asking questions to develop under-standing – in other words, thinking creatively. History helps pupils to understand the difficulty of people's lives, how people change and how to be more in tune with their own identities as well as others.

## Music

The building blocks for this subject are set out in 'Expressive Arts and Design' which provides opportunities and encouragement for sharing thoughts, ideas and feelings through a variety of activities in music, movement and dance. Music is a universal language and is a form of creative output. It can also provide opportunities for children to listen deeply and engage critically with music, sharing their opinions and learning about the skills behind the sounds they hear. Much creative thinking is involved in evaluating and creating music.

## Physical education (PE)

Physical development involves providing opportunities for young children to be active, to work with others and develop their coordination, control and movement. PE gives children a good start towards lifelong positive health and well-being as well as encouraging values such as fairness and respect.

## Personal, Social, Health and Economic (PSHE) education and relationships and health education

Personal, social, and emotional development in the Early Years involves helping children to develop confidence and a positive sense of themselves and others, form positive relationships rooted in respect and develop social skills including understand and managing behaviour. As of 2020, PSHE as an entire subject is not compulsory, shocking though this is. It has, however, become statutory to include relationships education and health education in primary schools. This is to help pupils to be 'happy health and safe' (DfE 2019). The DfE also state that schools **should** teach PSHE as a wider subject than just relationships and health, tailoring the curriculum to meet the needs of the students the school serves. The PSHE Association (https://www.pshe-association.org.uk) advocates a curriculum which encompasses three core themes which would support children well in social, moral spiritual and cultural aspects of learning:

- **Health and Well-Being** – physical and mental, social and emotional aspects of learning
- **Relationships** – respect for ourselves and others, having the confidence to make the right choices based on knowledge and sound understanding of risk
- **Living in the Wider World** – financial education to develop an understanding of where money comes from and how to manage personal finances and citizenship education to understand what it means to be part of a community in terms of how to behave and the ability to contribute positively to society

## Religious education

Religious education (RE) is not part of the National Curriculum, although, like PSHE, it is recognised as contributing to a broad and balanced curriculum and is developed at the local level. The aim of RE is to develop learners to enquire about, investigate and understand religions and beliefs. RE is a journey during which pupils should have the opportunity to explore questions of human existence and behaviour and questions of meaning and value. This subject provides opportunities, with reference to the specific beliefs and religions studied, for children to think about and interpret religious beliefs and teachings, sources of information including holy texts, practices of different religions including rites of passage and festivals and ways of life and of expressing meaning.

It is clear to see that there are many opportunities for creative thought in several of the subjects taught. In a letter to Sir Jim Rose, Education Minister Ed Balls (Parliament of the United Kingdom 2008) stated that the primary curriculum 'must provide all pupils with a broad and balanced entitlement to learning which encourages creativity and inspires in them a commitment to learning that will last a lifetime'. Note the reference not only to a broad and balanced curriculum but one which encourages creativity, this is at the core of the book you are reading! The Labour government's plans in 2009 for a new primary curriculum led to most schools, including the one I was working in at the time, to prepare for a curriculum that blended some of the foundation subjects into cross-curricular themed teaching and learning experiences. The topic-based or 'creative curriculum' was developed from Jim Rose's (2009) work suggesting the curriculum be organised into six broad areas of learning:

- Understanding English, communications and languages
- Mathematical understanding
- Scientific and technological understanding
- Historical, geographical and social understanding
- Understanding physical development, health and well-being
- Understanding the arts

Interestingly in a parallel independent study by the Cambridge Primary Review (2009), the team also suggested organising the curriculum into 'domains':

- Language, oracy and literacy
- Mathematics
- Science and technology
- Place and time

- Physical and emotional health
- Arts and creativity
- Citizenship and ethics
- Faith and belief

These changes never took place within the National Curriculum itself but are intrinsically linked in many school's planning documents and are the basis of grouping subjects, teaching them in tandem whilst leaving other subjects 'fallow' and picking them up at a later date where they fit with different 'domains'. You may be wondering why these changes never took place; this was certainly true of practitioners at the time who had spent time preparing and had even received copies of a glossy new document with an intertwined logo of colours symbolising the connections between the subjects. Ed Balls, the secretary of state for education at the time, announced proposals for a new national curriculum to come into force in September 2011. However, on 6 May 2010, the Labour government was succeeded by the Conservative and Liberal Democrat coalition government. The Department for Children, Schools and Families (DSCF) was replaced by the Department for Education (DfE), which announced on 7 June 2010 that it 'did not intend to proceed with the new primary curriculum' (Blair & Francis 2011).

During the academic year 2009–10, the Labour government's plans for a new primary national curriculum led schools to prepare for a new curriculum that blended some of the foundation subjects into cross-curricular, themed teaching and learning experiences.

This cross-curricular approach nonetheless makes sense to most primary practitioners as many skills taught in a particular subject domain cross over to others; this is clear to see in simple terms if we look at one small area of mathematics – handling data – and a single science skill – presenting findings from an investigation. Using the National Curriculum as a starting point, it is possible to make our own links and develop exciting and engaging lessons with a curricular theme. The interconnectivity of so many subjects, and thus the need for a broad and balanced curriculum, can be beautifully illustrated by an extract of a rich text such as 'Mountains of the Mind' by Robert Macfarlane (2003; see the following extract). The breadth of subjects studied can directly help or hinder the reading and understanding of a text:

We arrived in Zermatt in early June, hoping to climb the Matterhorn before the summer crowds clogged it up. But the mountain was still thickly armoured with ice: too dangerous for us to attempt. So we drove round to the next valley, where the thaw was supposed to be a little more advanced. Our plan was to camp high overnight, and then the following morning ascend a mountain called the Lagginhorn by its easy south-east ridge. At 4,010 metres, I reflected briefly, the Lagginhorn was almost exactly half the height of the Annapurna.

It snowed that night, and I lay awake listening to the heavy flakes falling onto the flysheet of our tent. They clumped together to make dark continents of shadow on the fabric, until the drifts became too heavy for the slope of the tent and slid with a soft hiss down to the ground. In the small hours the snow stopped, but when we unzipped the tent door at 6 a.m. there was an ominous yellowish storm light drizzling through the clouds. We set off apprehensively towards the ridge.

Once we were on it, the ridge turned out to be harder than it looked from below. The difficulty came from the old, rotten snow which was cloaking the ridge to a depth of several feet, together with six inches of fresh fall lying on top of it, uncompacted and sticky. Rotten snow is either granular, like sugar, or forms a crunchy matrix of longer, thinner crystals which have been hollowed out and separated from one another. Either way, it is unstable.

(Macfarlane 2003, p. 10)

There are many terms within this short excerpt which demonstrate the knowledge required to fully understand this text. I have analysed the following vocabulary to demonstrate: *Matterhorn* – geographical knowledge of what and where the Matterhorn is; *armoured* – historical knowledge to understand why this metaphor is an appropriate one to use; *4010 metres* – mathematical understanding of measure; *flysheet of our tent* – wider life experiences of having camped or at least been inside a tent; *soft hiss* – musical awareness to know what a 'hiss' is or equally experience of animals hissing; *6 a.m.* – mathematical knowledge of time to know that this is early in the morning, setting the scene; *yellowish* – art to know the colour yellow and variations of the same; and *granular like sugar* – science knowledge of the word *granular*' or cooking/baking experience.

This activity could be repeated with many excellent texts both with staff to highlight the need to teach a broad curriculum and with children to show one way in which we make connections and how their wider knowledge is brought together. What also resonated with me when reading this text was that experiences such as activity and adventure weeks, visitors coming into school and day trips including museum visits, theatre trips, picnics in the countryside or a day at the beach all enhance children's education and build a solid foundation for their future. This backed up one of my observations of an Early Years Forest School experience, where I noted the incredibly rich vocabulary being used, from asking a friend to pass a specific tool to describing in detail a minibeast they had found. There was mutual respect for their environment, the adults and each other, taking great care over their findings and demonstrating wonderful manners and the ability to share when it came to limited equipment. None of this was contrived; it was a vital requirement in order to fulfil the task, and because of this, the children were learning so much more than one singular skill.

A balanced curriculum is one where no single subject or experience dominates the timetable to the detriment of others. It could be argued that maths and English dominate the curriculum in most schools however it is important to remember that the skills taught in these two curriculum areas do enable access to the others. Alongside this we need to consider the breadth within the subjects to ensure progression throughout the primary phase, building on previous learning. An area of learning which particularly springs to mind is the humanities, history, geography, RE and PSHE. Within each of these subjects, there is a wealth of knowledge and skills identified in the National Curriculum, and, of course, beyond this, for children to be exposed to and to learn from. It would be perfectly possible (although undesirable) to hone in only on one timeframe in history or one area of geography, such as mapwork, or only on awareness of healthy choices in PSHE, regarding drugs and alcohol for example; however, this would limit the knowledge, skills and experiences children are exposed to over time and would not provide them with the breadth of knowledge needed to equip them for life and to be able to comprehend a text such as the one in Figure 5.1.

I hope that you can now see the rationale for a 'broad and balanced' curriculum. You may be wondering why it needs to be spelt out and who would narrow a curriculum or for what purpose. It is this scenario to which we now turn.

Having been a Year 6 teacher, I have felt the pressure of 'outcomes', specifically 'hitting targets'. Past emphasis has been placed on statistics of National Curriculum levels and the annual percentage increases regarding 'raising standards'. Despite my best intentions at the time, due to the pressure I was under, I have felt the need to focus my attention on those subjects being tested, which used to be maths, English and Science. This ultimately led to limited time to focus on the humanities, arts and music so I used to plan projects which focussed on these areas of the curriculum post Standard Attainment Tests. I was not alone; this was what was commonly known as 'narrowing the curriculum'. It was not advocated or celebrated but was felt necessary in order to spend time 'raising standards' in the subjects to be tested. In fact, Her Majesties Chief Inspector Amanda Spielman (2019) made note of this:

> we all know that too much weight placed on performance measures alone can lead to a degree of distortion, both in what is taught and not taught.
> Education is about more than exams … education is about something more.
>
> (Blair 1996 cited by Gillard 2018b)

Spielman (2017) was also clear in her discussions from curriculum research that '[a] good curriculum should lead to good results. However … [i]n the worst cases, teaching to the test, rather than teaching the full curriculum, leaves a pupil with a hollowed out and flimsy understanding'. She goes on to say that '[w]ithout receiving knowledge, pupils have learned nothing and no progress has been made – whatever the measures might indicate. This is why exams should exist in the service of the curriculum rather than the other way round' (Spielman 2017). This is crucial for schools to understand and to provide a rich and engaging curriculum with a vast breadth and depth of knowledge and skills. I agree with Spielman (2019) that '[i]f children know more, can do more, and remember more, then they have made progress'. However, I would also add 'make connections' to this definition.

As an Ofsted inspector and practitioner, I was delighted to see the shift to focus more on the 'Quality and Substance of Education', effectively what is taught and the impact it has, combining the previous areas of 'Teaching, Learning & Assessment' and 'Outcomes'. Spielman (2019) explains that outcomes do matter, of course, but these should be explored in the context of learning and as a result of that learning rather than in isolation, how assessment informs feedback and future planning and ultimately pupil progress. She also reassures practitioners, as I have said early on, that there is no need to develop a new curriculum from scratch and there is not a one-size-fits-all 'Ofsted approved curriculum'. Spielman clearly states that the frameworks already in place such as the National Curriculum and Early Years Foundations Stage Framework are solid bases from which to work.

In the Early Years, there is much to be proud of, and there are many elements which should not cease as children continue their primary school journey. To put this into perspective, I need to briefly outline the Early Years curriculum for those of you who are not so familiar with it. It is broken down into three areas of focus: prime areas, specific areas and characteristics of effective learning.

Prime areas are essential skills supporting progress in all other areas of learning, namely, personal, social and emotional development; communication and language; and physical development. The prime areas are key and should not be underestimated. Without these developmental milestones being supported and nurtured, children will find other areas of learning challenging beyond the Early Years. It is interesting to explore groups of children further up the school, say, in Years 4, 5 and 6, who need additional academic support or those on the special needs register to see who was identified as struggling to secure the prime areas of learning in the Early Years. Ask yourself if there was a lost opportunity in improving the prime areas of learning early on or if interventions in this area would make a difference now? This is something which should be tracked carefully and much earlier than Key Stage 2 so that interventions can be put in place to support children in these areas. Perhaps this is something you have carried out in your school; if so, it is certainly something to be proud of.

Then there are the specific areas of learning which more closely align to the National Curriculum subjects in Key Stages 1 and 2. These are literacy, maths, understanding the world and expressive arts and design.

Characteristics of effective learning explore the ways in which children connect with others and their environment. These traits can be broken down further in to playing and exploring (are they engaged, are they keen to 'have a go', do they play around with what they know and do they like to find things out for themselves?), active learning (how motivated and resilient they are, are they able to concentrate and do they enjoy and learn with purpose?) and creating and thinking critically (do they have original ideas, make links and choose methods?).

Critical or creative thinking is rightly a core component of what makes an effective learner, even for the youngest children in education. It starts right at the beginning. These characteristics should be nurtured throughout primary school; in a nutshell, we want all our learners to be engaged, motivated and creative thinkers. This should be at the forefront of any updated national curriculum and certainly feature heavily in a well-thought-out school curriculum, providing ample opportunities for children to hone these skills at age-appropriate levels.

Having highlighted a rich and diverse school curriculum under normal circumstances, 2020 presented us with anything but 'normal circumstances'. In March 2020, the entire school curriculum was disrupted despite the best efforts of school staff due to the COVID-19 pandemic and subsequent lockdowns. The first and third lockdowns caused all schools to close their doors to the majority of pupils (children of key workers and those most in need could still attend). Much of the learning had to take place remotely and teachers had to consider those with and without technology, resources and home support, as well as a range of ability needs. In the school I was working in at the time, we set work not only online but also provided paper copies for those without technology. We not only ensured 'challenges' were provided especially in maths and English for those children who thrive on further mental stimulation, but we also provided the option of a more accessible task for those who would usually have support in class but were now faced with working independently or with parents. There were celebrities providing online learning of all types, and some parents were opting to create their own curriculum from 'pick and mix' options available to them from PE lessons to baking and carrying out home tasks such as helping with cleaning the house, gardening and so on. There were a multitude of rich opportunities for many children such as 1:1 access to digital devices for some children able to make short movies of a particular learning experience or 1:1 support from a parent and a much quieter learning environment dramatically impacting on progress. However, much depended on home circumstances in terms of parental knowledge and the availability of resources, including the support of adults and a desire for parents to educate their own children, not something they had specifically set out to do but a situation many parents now found themselves in. All these contributing factors will have led to many inconsistencies in access to the same curriculum and levels of support. It is therefore important to explore how schools address these gaps. Advice from the UK government on fully re-opening schools after the first lockdown from March to July 2020 was to

> [t]each an ambitious and broad curriculum in all subjects from the start of the autumn term, but ... create time to cover the most important missed content ... prioritisation within subjects of the most important components for progression is likely to be more effective than removing subjects ... schools may consider how all subjects can contribute to the filling of gaps in core knowledge, for example through an emphasis on reading.

In other words, continue to teach a breadth of subjects but as a temporary measure, it is possible to streamline a subject and focus on key elements for one academic year. There is also a greater focus on utilising a cross-curricular approach ('consider how all subjects can contribute to filling gaps') to enhance efficiencies in ensuring a range of topics and key skills are taught. This adds more weight to the approach this book is advocating. There are many complexities involved with educating in a pandemic, and this is discussed in more detail in Chapter 10.

In Chapter 5, we delve into the terminology used by Ofsted – *intent, implementation* and *impact* – to understand the cycle of planning, delivery and knowing whether what we have put in place has been effective. It is in this chapter that I share teaching ideas from myself and colleagues to illustrate creativity and the interconnectedness of subject skills and knowledge.

---

- Is there a breadth of subject skills, knowledge and experiences within our school curriculum?
- Do we focus on one subject area more than another, and if so, why? Is our curriculum balanced?
- What does each subject look like in our school?
- Do we introduce a range of skills and knowledge at least in line with the National Curriculum, and do we go beyond this? If not, why not? (There may be a good reason or not!)
- Ask yourself if there was a lost opportunity in improving the prime areas of learning early on or if interventions in this area would make a difference to some learners now?

---

## Bibliography

Books and articles

Macfarlane R. (2003) *Mountains of the Mind: How Desolate and Forbidding Heights Were Transformed into Experiences of Indomitable Spirit*, London: Granta Publishers.

Journals and reports

Blair, E. & Francis, L. (2011) Was it right to abandon the creative curriculum? *Practical Research for Education, 44*, 26–32.

DfE & Gibb, N. (2015) *Speech: The purpose of education*, London: DfE Available from: https://www.gov.uk/government/speeches/the-purpose-of-education Accessed 19 February 2020.

DfE (2019) *Introduction: Relationships Education, Relationships and Sex Education (RSE) and Health Education* Available from: https://www.gov.uk/government/publications/changes-to-personal-social-health-and-economic-pshe-and-relationships-and-sex-education-rse/introduction-relationships-education-relationships-and-sex-education-rse-and-health-education Accessed 5 March 2020.

Early Education (2012) *Development Matters in the Early Years Foundation Stage (EYFS)* Available from: https://foundationyears.org.uk/files/2012/03/Development-Matters-FINAL-PRINT-AMENDED.pdf Accessed 17 March 2020.

Gillard, D. (2018a) *Jim Callaghan - Ruskin College speech (1976) Education in England: A history* Available from: http://www.educationengland.org.uk/documents/speeches/1976ruskin.html Accessed 6 July 2020.

Gillard, D. (2018b) *Tony Blair - Ruskin College speech (1996) Education in England: A history* Available from: http://www.educationengland.org.uk/documents/speeches/1996ruskin.html Accessed 6 July 2020

Parliament of the United Kingdom (2008) The Secretary of State for Children, Schools and Families (Ed Balls) *Written Ministerial Statements Wednesday 9 January Children, Schools and Families Primary Curriculum Review* Available from: https://publications.parliament.uk/pa/cm200708/cmhansrd/cm080109/wmstext/80109m0001.htm Accessed 5 January 2020.

Rose, J. (2009) *Independent Review of the Primary Curriculum: Final Report*, Nottingham: DCSF Publications. Available from: http://www.educationengland.org.uk/documents/pdfs/2009-IRPC-final-report.pdf Accessed 17 March 2020.

Spielman, A. (2017) *HMCI's commentary: recent primary and secondary curriculum research*, London: Ofsted. Available from: https://www.gov.uk/government/speeches/hmcis-commentary-october-2017 Accessed 10 March 2020.

Spielman, A. (2019) *Education inspection framework 2019: inspecting the substance of education – Foreword*, London: Ofsted. Available from: https://www.gov.uk/government/consultations/education-inspection-framework-2019-inspecting-the-substance-of-education/education-inspection-framework-2019-inspecting-the-substance-of-education Accessed 10 March 2020.

## Websites

https://www.pshe-association.org.uk
https://www.pshe-association.org.uk/curriculum

# Chapter 5

## Curriculum champions

- Who are the curriculum champions?
- What does the role of a subject leader entail?
- What is an 'action plan' and a 'deep dive'?
- How can we prioritise spending within subject budgets?

In Chapter 4, we examined the subjects which make up the curriculum and regardless of whether these are arranged by 'domains' or by subjects each area requires leadership and management. Leadership is required to inspire others, to support staff knowledge and skills and to keep abreast of new developments. Management is needed to ensure the coverage of key skills and knowledge by carefully tracking documents and monitoring the quality of teaching. Subject leaders must manage their allocated budget effectively and be champions of their subject area.

Effective curriculum leadership comes from the senior leaders in the first instance. Imagine all subject leaders simultaneously implementing improvements in their subject area. I doubt the improvements would be particularly effective when disseminated to overwhelmed class teachers having heard the same message from each subject leader! My advice to senior leadership is to take an overview of subjects and prioritise areas for development within a given time scale, for example over a four-year period. This enables a calm and focused approach as well as efficient allocation of funding. In one small school I have worked in, most foundation subjects were allocated £100 per year, which could achieve little; however, redistributing funds in conjunction with the curriculum development plan meant that some subjects received no budget at all for three years but, in the fourth year, would

DOI: 10.4324/9781003033189-5

Budget Model

| OLD MODEL | | Year A | | Year B | | Year C | | Year D | |
|---|---|---|---|---|---|---|---|---|---|
| Maths | £200.00 | Maths | £200.00 | Maths | £200.00 | Maths | £200.00 | Maths | £200.00 |
| English | £200.00 | English | £200.00 | English | £200.00 | English | £200.00 | English | £200.00 |
| Science | £100.00 | Science | £100.00 | Science | £350.00 | Science | £100.00 | Science | £100.00 |
| Design Technology | £100.00 | Design Technology | £100.00 | Design Technology | £350.00 | Design Technology | £100.00 | Design Technology | £100.00 |
| Art | £100.00 | Art | £100.00 | Art | £100.00 | Art | £350.00 | Art | £100.00 |
| Music | £100.00 | Music | £0.00 | Music | £0.00 | Music | £250.00 | Music | £0.00 |
| PHSE | £100.00 | PHSE | £0.00 | PHSE | £0.00 | PHSE | £0.00 | PHSE | £250.00 |
| History | £100.00 | History | £250.00 | History | £0.00 | History | £0.00 | History | £0.00 |
| Geography | £100.00 | Geography | £250.00 | Geography | £0.00 | Geography | £0.00 | Geography | £0.00 |
| RE | £100.00 | RE | £0.00 | RE | £0.00 | RE | £0.00 | RE | £250.00 |
| Sum of subject pots | £1,200.00 | Sum of subject pots | £1,200.00 | Sum of subject pots | £1,200.00 | Sum of subject pots | £1,200.00 | Sum of subject pots | £1,200.00 |

Figure 5.1: Curriculum budget model

receive a larger figure which could be used much more effectively on targeted resources, which would be able to be used across the school and would last for at least the next four years (Figure 5.1).

For the identified subjects each year, time should be allocated in staff meetings to raise the profile of this subject, sharing key information and training for staff. Money aligned from the staff training budget can be allocated to subject leader training for the priority curriculum subjects for that year.

Being a subject leader in a primary school is different to the role in a secondary school; the teacher does not always begin with specialist knowledge in their allocated subject, although there is usually an interest expressed or some background knowledge, unless, of course, you have just drawn the 'short straw'! In that case, the first role is to gen up on the subject as broadly as possible and specifically on the skills and knowledge primary-aged children need as well as any established and new developments in pedagogy within your subject. This important information should be shared with your colleagues through staff training and other communication methods, such as emails with links to any useful documents. Next you should identify the areas for development from the whole school development plan and, where necessary, seek support from staff in other schools, from training and reading subject matter. Having a solid knowledge base will enable you to inspire others, to purchase engaging and relevant resources and to suggest appropriate enhancements to the curriculum such as places to visit or which visitors to invite into the classroom for a high-quality learning experience, which is a key aspect of championing your subject and inspiring staff and children. An example of this from my own experience was a drama group that presented a 'science production', and I would say that the emphasis was far more on the entertainment and drama than it was on the science; suffice to say, they did not return! However, a group that did become regular visitors were the 'Explorer Dome'; the high-level science knowledge and the age-appropriate dissemination were always fantastic. The interactivity of the workshop was impressive and crawling into an inflated 'igloo' in the school hall made the experience even more exciting! I would almost always choose the 'light show' or 'space' as these were two areas which staff found challenging to teach in the class, especially because of the practicalities of blocking out enough natural light to carry out the experiments effectively.

In a nutshell, your role is to be the champion of your subject!

As the 'computing champion', I was acutely aware of the deficiencies of our provision and the limitations on our budget, but I was determined that our children deserved more than we were currently providing. To rectify this, I set up a charity along with some incredibly supportive and knowledgeable parents and reached out to the local council and businesses. Along with our charity fundraising, this resulted in the children having access to a bank of laptops and a bank of tablet devices. This improved the quality of teaching and learning as the devices worked effectively, were portable and could be relied on (which could not be said about the old desktop devices). The portability meant that we could use the devices in class and without the restriction of a single room; we were able to utilise them more effectively in other subjects for the application of computing skills. I am not suggesting that every subject leader sets up a charity to be able to afford the essentials, but it is often worth exploring other funding streams if a resource is worth having yet the budget is incredibly restricted.

Having identified areas of development in your subject aligned with the whole-school development plan, an 'action plan' or an 'impact evaluation plan' is a useful annual document. In this document, you will set out the intent, proposed implementation and anticipated impact for the academic year of a range of actions regardless of funding; however, it is likely to include more actions in the year it is in the spotlight with funding allocated. One addition I would make to this document is to facilitate a review at the end of the year so that you can evaluate whether the impact was as you had hoped as well as outlining next steps. This could be as notes overleaf or perhaps by highlighting in green if actions are complete, amber if continuing as a priority in the following year and red with annotation giving reasons if it should be discarded for the following year. The style of this document and the evaluation is personal to the way you work and any preferred methods in your school. A few examples (minus this evaluation) follow (Figures 5.2–5.4)

**Action Plan - Curriculum**

| Overarching Goal: | First Steps | Impact Lead: | Date: |
|---|---|---|---|
| Most children working at or beyond national standards at the end of Y2 and Y6 | • Monitor rigour of new NC through Long Term Plans for each subject | EP | September 2015 |

| FINAL OUTCOMES | INTERMEDIATE OUTCOMES | PLANNED ACTIONS | DATE FOR COMPLETION | RESOURCES |
|---|---|---|---|---|
| Over 85% achieving ARE by July 2016. | Gaps in learning are highlighted on tracking documents and used to inform planning. | Staff planning 3 units of work per year with a fun and engaging connector/theme meeting the needs of all learners. Staff highlighting curriculum coverage on LTP's in line with Creative Curriculum plans; both reviewed by Curriculum Coordinator. Parent overviews published for each unit and structured yet creative homework every 2 weeks. Targets highlighted for Maths, Reading and Writing for each child to track progress. | December 2015 | EP time to analyse data (3 x per year). EP time to analyse plans |
| Improvements in writing are evident through meeting ARE and the use of expressive language. | Opportunities for P4C in every class weekly. | Explore the use of Philosophy for Children (P4C) in some subjects (PSHCE and RWI to start) to deepen thinking skills and further challenge children with High Learning Potential (HLP) | December 2015 | Time for staff meeting: P4C. Time for pupil progress meetings. |
| Assessment information is consistent throughout the school | Assessment procedures are clear and applied by all. Staff confidence in assessing work is improved through monitoring meetings. | Staff meetings allocated to moderating writing and assessing maths from regular book scrutiny. Regular Pupil Progress meetings held to identify concerns. | Termly | Staff meeting time for moderation. Meeting time for EP and staff for Pupil Progress meetings |
| *EVIDENCE | *EVIDENCE | *EVIDENCE | | *EVIDENCE |
| Assessment information. Observations of learning. Pupil Voice | Provision Maps. Targets in books | Data analysis from EP. Staff meeting minutes and feedback from staff. Provision Maps. Itrack | | Diary/Blog of EP management time. Minutes of meetings |

Areas for future development: Produce Action Plan for Philosophy 4 Children as a cross curricular tool to develop a 'Thinking School' and continue to raise standards for ALL children.

Figure 5.2.: Curriculum action plan

**Action Plan - Computing 2015**

| Overarching Goal: | First Steps | | Impact Lead: | Date: |
|---|---|---|---|---|
| To equip young people with the foundational skills, knowledge and understanding of computing they will need for the rest of their lives. | • Share best practice of planning for the new NC in terms of high qualityLong Term Plans which include all three aspects of the new National Curriculum.<br>• Ensure a range of resources are available for use and staff are confident in using them. eg Purple Mash and other software on the network as well as hardware such as Log It, Microphones and cameras | | EP | September 2015 |

| FINAL OUTCOMES | INTERMEDIATE OUTCOMES | PLANNED ACTIONS | DATE FOR COMPLETION | RESOURCES |
|---|---|---|---|---|
| Pupils know how computers and computer systems work; they design and build programs, develop their ideas using technology and create a range of content. | Staff are confident in their delivery of Computer Science, and are familiar with a range of tools which enable pupils to design and debug programmes. | BE (external advisor) to work with staff on a rolling rota utilising such resources as 'Computer Science Unplugged', Purple Mash Coding, Scratch, and The Hour of Code resources including Light bot and others. | July 2016 | BE 'Computer Science Unplugged', Purple Mash Coding, Scratch, and The Hour of Code resources including Light bot and others. |
| Pupils select, use and combine a variety of Information technologies (software and hardware) across the curriculum to create, organise, store, manipulate, retrieve and present digital content | Staff are confident in their use of a range of software and hardware which enable children to create, organise, store, manipulate, retrieve and present digital content across the curriculum. | • Ensure ongoing access to hardware and software which are up to date and working effectively<br>• Audit Current Resources and clearly label to ensure accessibility for all staff and pupils.<br>• Create an Inventory stating the name and potential use for each resource<br>• Train staff in how to use unfamiliar technology | Ongoing<br><br>October 2015<br><br>October 2015<br><br>December 2015 | JWTechnical support<br><br>Time for EP/ BE to audit and create inventory of resources<br><br>Time allocated to staff meeting for training in use of software and hardware. (Recorded on the iPad as a movie for future reference) |
| Pupils demonstrate sound digital literacy in using technology safely, respectfully and responsibly and are discerning in evaluating digital content as the progress through the school. | All staff familiar with and utilise CEOPSresources including 'Think you know' | **EP to undertake Keeping Children Safe Online (KCSO) e-learning for professionals in order to train all stakeholders**<br>EP provide training on CEOPS resources and internet safety for staff, pupils and parents | January 2016 | EP 3 hours of time<br>(Use some of a Tue L&M day off site)<br>£20 to pay for training |
| *EVIDENCE<br>Networked pupil portfolios<br>Lesson Observations<br>Pupil Voice | *EVIDENCE<br>Networked pupil portfolios<br>Lesson Observations<br>Pupil Voice | *EVIDENCE<br>Learning Log recorded by BE--what was taught to whom<br>Resources inventory<br>Minutes from staff training / movie<br>Verification of staff subscription to CEOPS | | *EVIDENCE<br>Learning Log recorded by BE<br>Resources inventory<br>Minutes from staff training / movie<br>Invoice and minutes of external trainer |

Areas for future development:_ Utilise Digital Learning Platforms effectively for off-site learning

Figure 5.3: Computing action plan

**Action Plan for Extension and Enrichment-High Potential Learners**
(NB Evidence of Impact can be qualitative, quantitative or change as a result of intervention)

| Overarching Goal: | First Steps | | Impact Lead: | Date: |
|---|---|---|---|---|
| Most children working at or beyond national expectations at the end of Y2 and Y6 | • Staff access http://www.potentialplus.org | | EP | September 2015 |

| FINAL OUTCOMES | INTERMEDIATE OUTCOMES | PLANNED ACTIONS | DATE FOR COMPLETION | RESOURCES |
|---|---|---|---|---|
| Lesson observations by SLT and governors evidence inclusive approach to challenge. | Staff access http://www.potentialplusuk.org Join school as a member to access further advice and support (funding permitting) | Staff meeting to access http://www.potentialplusuk.org and discuss ideas to challenge children (Expires Dec '15 –renew) Share model of Growth Mindset and develop autonomous learning through pupil choice. EP and FW to share approach to teaching. Monitor lessonsto ensure provision for children with HLP is evident | (early) November 2015 | Time for staff meeting Access to http://www.potentialplusuk.org (see itslearning for link) Funding £265 for 3 years (£88.33 pa) |
| Teachers plan a range of groupings which vary according to (amongst other things) learning style which enable pupils to be challenged. | Staff aware of 'Learning Styles' and know how to cater for a variety of styles | EP to run a workshop on 'Higher Order challenges' (Problem solving and Mastery) where teachers carry out literary research during the session and feedback ideas to the group. Staff then trial a range of approaches and share best experiences at next meeting. | December 2015 | Time EP to prepare meeting and Time to gather some documents to explore further |
| Most able children are challenged in all areas of the curriculum but especially reading and writing so they do not 'coast'. | Children with HLP are challenged in lessons and those underachieving are identified on provision maps for rapid improvement | Pupil Progress meetings will continue to identify children with HLP and those who are potential underachievers within this category | Termly reviews | Time for pupil progress meetings |
| Pupils discuss deeply, show greater tolerance of one another and have a wide vocabulary for expressing thought sand ideas. | Staff plan to use P4C approach once a week in a lesson of choice to develop this way of thinking. | EP to recap Philosophy for Children (P4C) as a way of working and share notes from before on the potential across other subjects. Staff use time to plan another session. | January 2016 | Time EP to prepare meeting and Time for staff meeting on P4C |
| *EVIDENCE | *EVIDENCE | *EVIDENCE | | *EVIDENCE |
| Lesson observations Planning docs Most Able children continue to develop academically especially in Literacy P4C session plans and observations | Assessment information (including vulnerable groups) Provision Maps Presentations/notes from staff meetings | Data analysis Provision Maps Itrack Lesson obs for HLP provision Presentations/notes from staff meetings | | Minutes of meetings Reference to HLP strategies in lesson planning |

Areas for future development_Develop Philosophy 4 Children as a cross curricular tool to develop a 'Thinking School' and continue to raise standards for ALL children.

Figure 5.4: Extension and Enrichment action plan

The action plan should illustrate your school's intent for the subject, how it is implemented and the impact of teaching which will support you as a middle leader to drive progress in your subject. It will also be a useful aid to refer to during a 'deep dive' conversation with an inspector. A 'deep dive' is a way of triangulating information about the curriculum. Triangulation is the practice of collecting enough evidence from a range of sources to provide a secure evidence base, in Ofsted's case, for a judgement on the school's effectiveness. The inspectors will start with a conversation about the whole curriculum offer with senior leaders; they will discuss curriculum content and sequencing (intent) with subject leaders and then, through the deep dive, explore how this ties up with earlier discussions. The 'deep dives' consist of a range of inspection activities: lesson visits, work scrutiny and discussions with pupils and teachers across the school within the same subject. Consider with work scrutiny the time of year (this may be of limited use at the start of an academic year), the amount of work recorded in books (does this subject lend itself to recording on paper or is learning primarily expressed through drama/discussion/construction?) and the age of the learners will need to be taken into account; younger learners may have less recorded in books with a much more practical approach to learning, some of which may be recorded as a paper or electronic learning profile comprising photographs and adult observations. With all this taken into account, it can be a useful piece of evidence to demonstrate previous learning being used, it can certainly document whether the curriculum is being covered over time and it can point to issues with teaching approaches too. Inspectors will be looking to see intent, implementation and impact in action and linking that back to the bigger picture for the whole curriculum, this will often be done in conjunction with the subject leader. These 'deep dives' will be carried out across a range of subjects to see how it all links back to the overall intent for the curriculum in your school: Is there consistency within and across subjects? Are there any areas of concern in one specific area or is it a wider issue? Ofsted's (2019) paper 'Inspecting the Curriculum' explains that the purpose of the deep dive is to 'form an accurate evaluation of how education flows from intention to implementation to impact within a school'. It also states that inspection judgements on the quality of education must be based on 'the education that pupils are actually receiving … rather than simply being about ambitions or intentions'. When you are looking at work or visiting a lesson to explore intent, look backwards and forwards. Look backwards to explore whether building blocks were in place for children to understand what is currently being taught whether that is earlier in the lesson, topic or in the current academic year. Perhaps an observation might highlight gaps earlier in a child's learning journey which could be explained by a long absence because of illness, a pandemic which affected an entire year group or weak teaching? This weak teaching could be due to a lack of clarity about what the learning objective for the lesson is or weak subject knowledge. If this is identified early on and support put in place, this should have minimal impact on the children; however, if it is identified that the gaps are from previous academic years and which was not addressed soon enough, this may have a much larger effect possibly on an entire cohort. The questions which should be asked include, Has this now been addressed in terms of the teacher's knowledge, and have pupils' gaps in understanding been plugged with effective interventions? When looking forwards think about how this knowledge and understanding, as well as skills, are preparing children for their next steps in learning in the lesson, during the topic, year and in their longer-term future.

In writing this book, I hope by now you are aware that it is not a 'what Ofsted wants' text! However, what Ofsted does want is what is best for the children in your school, and I am sure that this is what every member of staff wants too. In addition to ensuring the rigour of your subject, it is good practice as a middle or senior leader to carry out your own deep dives for all subjects, and areas such as reading and spelling, in your school. Otherwise, how can you be sure of the quality of education your pupils are receiving, despite your best intentions? Your action plan identifies your intentions for your subject and what you expect to see in terms of implementation. Now you need to collect evidence to measure the impact. Go and visit lessons and make notes: Did you see what you hoped to? Does it align with your action plan? Gather in a sample of books about five or six from each class from a range of abilities and look at them in detail: How does this evidence the intent and what is the impact of your overarching goal to date? Where are you on the journey? Take some time out to talk to pupils and think carefully beforehand about what questions you want to not only ask to gather evidence to measure the impact of your action plan but also be open to hear things you were not expecting: What does that tell you? Are you going in the right direction, or does something need to change as a result? Have similar discussions and reflections with staff. In this way, you will be aware of what is working well and what needs to change. You will be able to communicate this to senior leadership, governors and Ofsted. More important, in carrying out these activities and evaluating the impact against your intent, you are having a positive impact on the children in your school by ensuring high-quality teaching and learning in your subject area.

As a curriculum leader, another of the roles is to ensure that the coverage of the curriculum is rigorous. Deep dives will help with this in terms of topics covered in books and lessons observed. Another tool to use is long-term and medium-term planning. A long-term plan sets out what is to be covered throughout the academic year and can be organised by year group or by subject. Having both formats is helpful for different audiences: by year group, they help the class teacher, and by subject, they support the curriculum leader, and it is this subject document I am referring to here. Some schools predetermine what is taught when, indicating this with termly headings on the plan; however, removing these headings can open opportunities for greater flexibility, creativity and pupil involvement. For example children choose the curriculum driver/connector/theme and the teacher plans for that. It encourages variety year on year and taps into the interest of the children in the class at that time. I would suggest collecting a bank of ideas from the class before the start of a new term and explaining that you will select from their suggestions (this enables you to select from a theme which best fits with the objectives you want to cover). Without termly headings, it is helpful to highlight which objectives have been covered using a colour code for each term: orange for autumn, green for spring and yellow for summer. This enables the subject coordinators to identify any gaps and to triangulate this document to evidence in student's books and lesson observations. The detail will be shown in a medium-term plan as to what objectives and wider opportunities will be covered in a particular unit of work. This is likely to also show the activities and resources required as well as support and extension activities. For many experienced teachers, this will be enough, although I used to like a daily overview so that I could scribble down any organisational notes and an aide memoir for resources I would need. For less experienced teachers, a short-term plan in the form of a lesson plan may be useful so that even more detail can be recorded on paper so as not to be overlooked. A lesson plan should be written for the person using it, however, and not for a wider audience.

Curriculum leadership and management require a range of skills in promoting the subject, upskilling staff and monitoring the quality of teaching and learning as well as managing the budget. It is also part of the jigsaw of the whole school curriculum. The stronger the individual pieces, the better they all fit together and the more robust the overall picture.

---

- Do we have a clear picture of what our school curriculum looks like in terms of intent, implementation and impact?
- How does this overarching view of our school curriculum translate into different subjects?
- What are our strengths and weaknesses, and what are we doing to resolve the issues arising?
- What order are we teaching in, and why?
- How do we decide on enrichment activities?

---

## Bibliography

### Journals and reports

Ofsted (2019) *Inspecting the Curriculum* Available from: https://www.gov.uk/government/publications/inspecting-the-curriculum Accessed 26 November 2020.

### Websites

http://www.explorerdome.co.uk/

# Chapter 6

## A creative curriculum for all

- What do we mean by 'all'?
- What different groups are there?
- What specific challenges are there for children with a particular characteristic?
- How can a creative curriculum support each child?

So far, assuming you are reading this book in a linear fashion, rather than dipping in and out, you understand more about the broad and balanced curriculum, about why creativity is vital and about the importance that each individual subject holds as part of the whole curriculum. In this chapter, we study how children are first and foremost unique individuals but that they also fall into categories depending on a range of factors; many children will fall into several 'groups' simultaneously. In exploring the intent and implementation of the curriculum through the lens of each of these groups, we should leave no child behind in terms of impact. This is what is meant by 'a creative curriculum for all' (Figure 6.1).

### Boys/Girls

For the purposes of this chapter, gender refers to the gender assigned at birth; however, as some people identify as non-binary from an early age, I wonder whether we will continue to compare children by their gender in the future.

Figure 6.1 shows the end of Key Stage 2 results for boys and girls (DfE 2019). (This was the most recent data at the time of writing due to the pandemic.) What we can see here is that boys are generally achieving at levels below girls but most significantly for reading, writing and grammar, punctuation and spelling. This trend

DOI: 10.4324/9781003033189-6

**Attainment and progress scores (with confidence intervals) by gender England, 2019 (all schools)**

| | Boys | Girls | Difference |
|---|---|---|---|
| **Reaching the expected standard** | | | |
| Reading, writing and maths | 60% | 70% | +10pp |
| Reading test | 69% | 78% | +9pp |
| Maths test | 78% | 79% | +1pp |
| GPS test | 74% | 83% | +9pp |
| Writing TA | 72% | 85% | +12pp |
| | | | |
| **Progress Scores** | | | |
| Reading | −0.5 (−0.5 to −0.6) | 0.6 (0.6 to 0.6) | +1.2 |
| Writing | −0.7 (0.7 to 0.8) | 0.8 (0.8 to 0.8) | +1.6 |
| Maths | 0.7 (0.7 to 0.7) | −0.7 (−0.7 to −0.7) | −1.4 |

Figure 6.1: Attainment and progress scores 2019
Source: National pupil database.

continues for progress. This is the impact of what has been implemented. It is very important, then, that through a creative curriculum we provide exciting and engaging opportunities for reading and writing which particularly inspire boys. This is not to say that they should be male-oriented themes such as football, cars or dinosaurs as this is the opposite of what we want to achieve. This is gender stereotyping and, in fact, contributes to the perception that boys can only write about specific topics. Experiential learning provides rich experiences for both boys and girls; if children have experienced walking on a beach or planting seeds for example, they can utilise these experiences to write about them; otherwise, they will find it much more of a challenge. As teachers, we should also be very mindful of gender equality and think about celebrating characters who defy traditional stereotypes rather than those who engender them. Historically, girls have achieved below boys in maths; however, barriers which previously prevented equal attainment levels have since been broken down, and girls are achieving similar levels. In terms of progress, however, this is not the case; goal setting, resilience and perseverance leading to sustained improvement are things to be explored further with girls to support an improvement in their progress.

## Special Educational Needs (SEN)

The Special Educational Needs and Disability Code of Practice states that a child or young person has Special Educational Needs (SEN) 'if they have a learning difficulty or disability which calls for special educational provision to be made for him or her … has a significantly greater difficulty in learning than the majority of others of the same age, has a disability which prevents or hinders him or her from making use of facilities of a kind generally provided for others of the same age in mainstream schools'.

(DfE 2015a)

If they are under school age but are likely to fall within the definition, they are also classed as having SEN (Children and Families Act 2014). Many children and young people who have SEN may have a disability under the Equality Act 2010 – that is 'a physical or mental impairment which has a long-term and substantial adverse effect on their ability to carry out normal day-to-day activities'.

Pupils with disabilities and those with SEN will often need adaptations to their learning through larger print, different coloured paper or additional resources, such as visual cues or apparatus; this may also be in the form of additional adult support. Creative tasks engage everyone so long as we consider their additional needs. For children who are identified as 'Gifted and Talented' or those with 'High Learning Potential' (a definition I have adopted from Potential Plus UK), they are likely to require additional challenges to maintain their engagement; they will benefit from opportunities to develop 'little c' creative thinking 'outside the box' to solve problems. A creative curriculum opens these opportunities to everyone, which avoids latent potential being otherwise missed. Unless opportunities are presented to children, it is difficult to identify who is gifted in a particular area of maths for example or talented at fashioning something extraordinary out of clay. If a wide range of creative opportunities are offered to everyone, it can highlight otherwise hidden geniuses, and if these opportunities are provided regularly, then those who do not find them naturally easy will be able to develop the skills over time.

## Black and minority ethnic groups

Ethnic groups are communities of people who share attributes which distinguish them from other groups, such as their traditions, language, culture, ancestry or religion. The most recent Census, in 2011, highlights that in England and Wales, 80 per cent of the population was white British, meaning that other ethnic groups were in the minority in the UK at this time; however, the minority ethnic group or groups in your school may look very different to the UK population as a whole and should be carefully considered.

It is important to ensure that the resources we use represent the children in our school community and the UK in general. If the stories we read and the textbooks or posters we see contain characters and images not related to our own cultures and experiences, it can give the subliminal message that we don't matter or that this educational diet is not for us. I cannot imagine any educator intentionally wanting this message to be heard. A creative curriculum lends itself to links being made across subjects, countries and cultures and should not only include the communities represented within your school but also ensure that children are made aware of the lives of people from other ethnic groups they might not encounter in school. This will help prepare them for life in modern Britain and build tolerance, respect and understanding of people who hold beliefs and values different from their own.

## Gypsy/Roma/Traveller (GRT)

GRT is used as an umbrella term embracing all Gypsy and Traveller groups. According to the Traveller Movement (2019), 'Gypsies have been in Britain since at least 1515 after migrating from continental Europe during the Roma migration from India. … The term Gypsy comes from "Egyptian" which is what the settled population perceived them to be because of their dark complexion.' *Roma* is a generic term used to describe many different groups of Romani(y) people. Spinelli (2012) explains that the Romani(y) population comprises five large groups from all over the world:

Roma: In Europe, mainly in the Balkans and in Central–Eastern Europe
Sinti: In the northern areas of Western Europe, in France and in Northern Italy
Kale or Cale: Meaning "black," in Finland, Wales, Spain, Portugal, Brazil, Algeria and
     Iraq
Manouches: France and Italy
Romanichals or Romaniche or Romany: England, North America and Australia

Some Traveller groups are known as 'cultural' rather than 'ethnic' Travellers, such as those who travel for work or are associated with fairs and the circus. They generally settle in one place over winter to repair any machinery or equipment and then travel in the summer months. 'New Travellers', derived from the hippie movements of the 1960s and 1970s, are those who don't have a long history of travelling in their family but have chosen this lifestyle for themselves. Barge Travellers, living on the waterways, can be seen as a branch of these 'New Travellers'.

'Evidence shows that children from Gypsy, Roma and Traveller backgrounds are among the lowest achieving groups at every key stage of education' (UK Parliament 2020). They also point out that this will only have been exacerbated during the pandemic due to limited access to digital devices and connectivity for online learning. According to the Department for Education (DfE), the low achievement is due to a complex range of factors, including barriers preventing full access to the curriculum such as lack of engagement, interrupted education and negative experiences of school (Wilkin et al. 2010). Some GRT parents have had limited and often negative school experiences; they sometimes therefore prioritise children's physical and moral safety and practical skills above academic achievement. A creative curriculum can support children from the GRT group by being a positive and engaging way to learn, as well as enable, the application of knowledge, skills and understanding across the curriculum and beyond into the practical life skills required for their future.

## Young carers

The carers trust defines a young carer as 'someone under 18 who helps look after someone in their family, or a friend, who is ill, disabled, has a mental health condition or misuses drugs or alcohol'. One in eight of the 177,918 young carers in England and Wales were identified by the 2011 Census as being younger than 8, and the Children's Society says that some are as young as 5 (Hounsell 2013)! They might be carrying out practical tasks in running a home; physical, emotional, medical or personal care; helping to look after siblings; or any combination of these.

'Around 40% of carers have high levels of anxiety or depression, with young carers known to have a prevalence of self-harm' (Wong 2017). Clay et al. (2016) reported the challenges young carers face in balancing caring and schoolwork, managing feelings of preoccupation, difficulty concentrating in class, limited time for homework and missing school days to provide care at home. It is vitally important that we ensure our school curriculum makes space for well-being and mental health support. This links back to the importance of a broad and balanced curriculum with subjects, such as sport, art and music, and creative outlets that enable children to express their emotions as well as Personal, Social, Health and Economic classes to support them with strategies for managing their mental health and knowing where to go for further help should it be required.

## Those with attendance issues

Regular and punctual attendance of pupils at schools is, under section 7 of the Education Act 1996, a legal requirement: 'If a child of compulsory school age who is a registered pupil at a school fails to attend regularly at the school, his parent is guilty of an offence.' This could be term-time absence, for example unauthorised holidays, or irregular attendance. Attendance issues are usually specific to the individual; it could be for example due to the child being a young carer, due to an ongoing medical issue, due possibly bullying or even a safeguarding issue. It is important that schools look closely at the complex reasons behind poor attendance and addresses them to ensure all pupils receive regular access to learning. There may be extenuating circumstances which explain the absence and schools are often in a good place to support families and signpost to a social worker when this is deemed appropriate. Since March 2020, many children have not physically attended the school building due to the COVID-19 pandemic; however, the term *attendance* has been redefined, and it is more about children participating in learning whether on-site, at home online or on paper and via telephone well-being conversations in some schools. This 'attendance' has been continually monitored in order to best support the children.

An engaging creative curriculum with exciting opportunities will encourage most children to attend school. They really want to learn and for those with more complex reasons for absence a more personalised approach is necessary.

## Those known to social services or who have a child protection plan

Children 'known to social services' mean that their parents or carers require some level of support to care for their child. A child protection plan is in place to protect the child from the risk of significant harm.

It is likely that these children will require mental health support and a school curriculum which encompasses mental health and well-being strategies will support a number of children in a range of challenging situations. Staff should also be mindful with family-related activities such as 'Mother's Day' or 'Father's Day' as this can bring up challenging feelings, especially if the child has been adopted or is in foster care.

## Pupils with medical needs

A new duty came into force to ensure that all children with medical conditions, both physical and mental, are properly supported 'so that they can play a full and active role in school life, remain healthy and achieve their academic potential' (DfE 2014). Children may be conscious of their medical condition and suffer anxiety as a result, and they may have long periods of absence for treatment, which can be quite unsettling and make re-integrating with the class challenging. This group of children can fall into the Special Educational Needs and Disabilities category and 'those with attendance issues'; however, the absences of these children should be dealt with sensitively since this is intrinsically linked to their condition.

A curriculum which promotes positive mental health strategies is going to be of benefit for children with medical needs as well as many other groups I have already mentioned. In addition, these children are likely to need support with managing their medical needs in school and developing independence at age age-appropriate levels such as children with diabetes learning to test their blood sugar level and administer their insulin or a child with asthma knowing when and how to use their inhaler.

## English as an additional language

A pupil is recorded as having English as an additional language if she/he is exposed to a language at home that is known or believed to be other than English. It is not a measure of English language proficiency.

(DfE 2020)

It is worth considering that the child will be learning in a language which may be unfamiliar to them if they have recently arrived in the country; however, they may be proficient in the language, and some technical vocabulary and idioms are likely to be unfamiliar and need additional support. Not only is the language itself a possible barrier to learning, but learning the culture may also be quite different and pedagogically unfamiliar. With the right support, all children can flourish within the framework of a creative curriculum, demonstrating their ability to think independently, question deeply and solve problems.

## Disadvantaged pupils

Disadvantaged pupils are those who without additional funding and support would be unfairly disadvantaged from their peers. This includes pupils who are eligible for free school meals, children with a member of their family in the services or who has retired from the Ministry of Defence and children who are looked after by the Local Authority or who have been adopted or have a special guardianship or child arrangement order.

'Evidence shows that children from disadvantaged backgrounds: generally face extra challenges in reaching their potential at school and often do not perform as well as their peers' (DfE 2021). The pupil premium to support disadvantaged pupils is not based on ability however, and those who are disadvantaged and able most often underperform as they are sadly in some cases overlooked for support in terms of building confidence and attempting more challenging tasks. In addition, children from service families especially, but other groups as well, may benefit more from pastoral rather than academic support or in conjunction with it. It is up to schools to manage the support in place. A creative curriculum which supports individuals and encourages critical and reflective thinking will support every learner. 'Good teaching is the most important lever schools have to improve outcomes for disadvantaged pupils' (Education Endowment Foundation 2011).

## Pupils in danger of radicalisation and extremism

As stated in the *Prevent* strategy,

> [r]adicalisation refers to the process by which a person comes to support terrorism and forms of extremism leading to terrorism. ... Extremism is vocal or active opposition to fundamental British values, ... or calls for the death of members of our armed forces.'
>
> (UK Parliament 2011)

The DfE (2015) explain that 'there is no single way of identifying an individual who is likely to be susceptible to a terrorist ideology'. This falls under a school's safeguarding duties, and changes in behaviour are likely to alert staff to a child who requires interventions to keep them safe. Some children may be very vocal about their views whilst others will keep them hidden.

A broad and balanced curriculum will not shy away from challenging conversations and, in fact, will provide a safe space for children to build on or challenge other people's viewpoints in a respectful way. Philosophy for Children is one approach in which children do not seek to win an argument but to discuss their own views and listen carefully to those of others to reach their own reasoned conclusion. Simply encouraging children to listen and respond to others in a supportive manner with sentence stems, such as 'I agree with X because … and I also think …' or equally, 'I disagree with X because … although …', and learning to respect and value differences of opinion is an invaluable tool for all children both for the here and now and in the future. PSHE encourages children to learn more about themselves and others in terms of cultural and social differences and similarities as well as understand and nurture self-esteem and mental well-being. Fundamental British values, including democracy, the rule of law, individual liberty and mutual respect and tolerance of different faiths and beliefs, should be woven through the curriculum to prepare children for life in modern Britain.

## Asylum seekers

> Asylum Seekers are people who flee their home country and seek refugee status in another country, possibly because of war or human rights abuses, and then lodge an application for asylum with the UK Government.
>
> (Rutter 2001)

Children who are asylum seekers will fall into several of the groups we have already explored; there is likely to be significant trauma in these children's lives, and they will benefit from mental health support not only in terms of specialist support but also in PSHE lessons within the curriculum. A creative curriculum can be effectively used to explore different themes and topics which are relevant to the children in your school. Expressive arts can also be very therapeutic, and yet again, I highlight the importance of a broad and balanced curriculum to ensure that children's needs are being met.

## Children who have been excluded or are at risk of exclusion

Persistent behavioural problems are the most common reason for exclusion or those at risk. These behaviours are a form of communication and should be carefully explored before a child is issued with a fixed term or permanent exclusion.

Children who are most likely to be excluded fall into several categories mentioned earlier; for example research has shown that boys are more likely to be excluded than girls, and children with special educational needs or mental health needs may also be at risk, especially if their needs are not being met. It is crucial therefore that we address the needs of children in each of the groups identified so that we can mitigate the exclusion of children from school.

A well-thought-out, broad and balanced curriculum with well-being, critical thinking and creative opportunities at its heart will scaffold the needs of all learners. It will do this by supporting learners to develop a strong sense of self and self-esteem, knowing how to nurture their well-being and being able to listen carefully to different viewpoints before thinking creatively to formulate their own beliefs through convergent and divergent thinking, exploring and critically evaluating what they know and have heard from a range of sources.

In the next chapter, we look at what is meant by Curriculum Intent, Implementation and Impact, new vocabulary introduced by Ofsted. Studying this should help you further understand curriculum.

---

- Which groups of children are the 'vulnerable groups' in your school?
- How do you know this?
- How are you ensuring no child is left behind?

---

## Bibliography

### Books and articles

Spinelli, S. (2012) *Rom, genti libere ["The Roma, Free People"]*, Milan: Dalai pp. 158–159  https://sfi.usc.edu/education/roma-sinti/en/conosciamo-i-roma-e-i-sinti/chi-sono/un-mondo-di-mondi/rom-sinti-kale-manouches-romaniche.php

### Journals and reports

Clay et al. (2016) *The lives of young carers in England Qualitative report to DfE February 2016* Online: DfE Available from: https://assets.publishing.service.gov.uk/government/uploads/system/uploads/attachment_data/file/498115/DFE-RR499_The_lives_of_young_carers_in_England.pdf Accessed 12 October 2020.

DfE (2014) Last updated (2017) *Supporting pupils with medical conditions at school* Online: DfE Available from: https://www.gov.uk/government/publications/supporting-pupils-at-school-with-medical-conditions--3 Accessed 6 March 2020.

DfE (2015a) *Special educational needs and disability code of practice: 0 to 25 years* Online: DfE Available from: https://assets.publishing.service.gov.uk/government/uploads/system/uploads/attachment_data/file/398815/SEND_Code_of_Practice_January_2015.pdf Accessed 6 March 2020.

DfE (2015b) *The Prevent Duty Departmental advice for schools and childcare providers* Online: DfE Available from: https://assets.publishing.service.gov.uk/government/uploads/system/uploads/attachment_data/file/439598/prevent-duty-departmental-advice-v6.pdf Accessed 23 February 2021.

DfE (2019) *National curriculum assessments at Key Stage 2 in England, 2019 (revised)* Available from: https://assets.publishing.service.gov.uk/government/uploads/system/uploads/attachment_data/file/851798/KS2_Revised_publication_text_2019_v3.pdf Accessed 6 July 2020.

DfE (2020) *English proficiency of pupils with English as an additional language* Online: DfE Available from: https://assets.publishing.service.gov.uk/government/uploads/system/uploads/attachment_data/file/868209/English_proficiency_of_EAL_pupils.pdf Accessed 6 March 2020.

DfE (2021) *Policy paper: Pupil premium* Online DfE Available from: https://www.gov.uk/government/publications/pupil-premium/pupil-premium Accessed 23 February 2021.

Education Endowment Foundation (2011) *The EEF Guide to the Pupil Premium* Online: EEF Available from: https://educationendowmentfoundation.org.uk/public/files/Publications/Pupil_Premium_Guidance.pdf Accessed 6 August 2020.

Hounsell (2013) *Hidden from view: The experiences of young carers in England* Online: The Children's Society Available from: https://www.childrenssociety.org.uk/sites/default/files/202010/hidden_from_view_final.pdf Accessed 12 October 2020.

Parliament of the United Kingdom (2011) *Secretary of State for the Home Department Prevent Strategy*, London: The Stationery Office Available from: https://assets.publishing.service.gov.uk/government/uploads/system/uploads/attachment_data/file/97976/prevent-strategy-review.pdf Accessed 5 January 2021

Parliament of the United Kingdom (2020) *Ministry of Housing, Communities & Local Government (Stephen Greenhalgh) Press release - Gypsy, Roma and Traveller children and young people to get extra education support* Available from: https://www.gov.uk/government/news/gypsy-roma-and-traveller-children-and-young-people-to-get-extra-education-support Accessed 5 January 2021.

Parliament of the United Kingdom (2014) *Children and Families Act 2014 Part 3 point 20* Available from: https://www.legislation.gov.uk/ukpga/2014/6/section/20/enacted Accessed 5 January 2021.

Parliament of the United Kingdom (1996) *Education Act 1996 Part 6 Chapter 2 School attendance* Available from: https://www.legislation.gov.uk/ukpga/1996/56/section/444 Accessed 6 August 2020.

Parliament of the United Kingdom (2010) *Equality Act 2010* Available from: https://www.legislation.gov.uk/ukpga/2010/15/contents Accessed 6 August 2020.

Rutter, J. (2001) *Educating Asylum Seeking and Refugee Children Guidance on the education of asylum seeking and refugee children* Online: DfEE Available from: https://dera.ioe.ac.uk/4925/1/EducatAsylumSeeking.pdf Accessed 5 January 2021.

The Traveller Movement (2019) *A Good Practice Guide for improving outcomes for Gypsy, Roma and Traveller Children in education*, London: The Traveller Movement Available from: https://travellermovement.org.uk/phocadownload/TTM%20Good%20Practice%20Guide%20Education_web.pdf Accessed 6 August 2020.

Wilkin, A. et al. (2010) *Improving the outcomes for Gypsy, Roma and Traveller pupils: final report*, London: DfE Available from: https://assets.publishing.service.gov.uk/government/uploads/system/uploads/attachment_data/file/181669/DFE-RR043.pdf Accessed 12 October 2020.

Wong, S. (2017) Young carers in the NHS. *The British Journal of General Practice: The Journal of the Royal College of General Practitioners*, 67(664), 527–528. Available from: https://www.ncbi.nlm.nih.gov/pmc/articles/PMC5647913/ Accessed 12 October 2020.

## Websites

https://travellermovement.org.uk/about/gypsy-roma-traveller-history-and-culture
https://carers.org/about-caring/about-young-carers
https://p4c.com/about-p4c/
https://potentialplusuk.org/

# Chapter 7

## Intent, implementation and impact

- What is meant by 'curriculum intent'?
- How is a curriculum implemented?
- How is impact measured?
- What are your own reflections on current practice in your own school?
- Ideas and examples of exciting and engaging lessons and ways to keep parents informed of learning are included to stimulate your own thoughts.

Having explored the history and purpose of curriculum, understood more about a broad and balanced curriculum and allocated some time to reflect at the end of Chapter 2, let us now examine curriculum in more detail. We will do this through the terminology Ofsted (2019) have used over the last couple of years, using the concepts of 'intent', 'implementation' and 'impact' to 'recognise that the curriculum passes through different states: it is conceived, taught and experienced. All these steps are connected; they relate back to my undergraduate learning of lesson planning: 'plan, do, review'. There needs to be a clear plan so that you are sure about what it is you are teaching and what you hope the learners will gain from the experience, it then needs to be taught and, of course, in order to know if you have met your aims, there needs to be a review process. This is true at the individual lesson level and of the entire curriculum. Although the mechanics are the same, it will look different at the higher level, and it is this I focus on in this chapter. For the sake of deeper analysis, I am breaking each of the components down so that we can explore each in turn; that is not to say one element is more important than the other or can stand in isolation.

DOI: 10.4324/9781003033189-7

## Intent

*Aim*, *objective* or *purpose* are three synonyms which could easily replace *intent*, and for me, the word *purpose* fits best: What is the purpose of teaching what we propose to teach? In other words, 'why?' Why are we teaching it, and in why in the particular chosen order? During my early years as a teacher, I am ashamed to say that this question never crossed my mind. I just taught in a robotic manner, following the National Curriculum objectives, school schemes and more or less 'did as I was told' by school leadership. I suppose this is unsurprising given my limited experience, and we all have to start somewhere! It was during my MA in education when we were exploring the origins of 'curriculum' that I thought more deeply about the purpose of what I was teaching and why it was important. This is where my passion for 'creative curriculum' came from and later within my role as deputy head as the leader of 'curriculum development'. Ofsted is clear that when it defines *intent*. It means '[l]eaders and teachers design, structure and sequence a curriculum' (Ofsted 2019). This is the concept of the 'craft' of teaching, it is where creativity begins; in the design, structure and sequencing, through exploring the needs of the children the school serves and to create exciting opportunities. The key inclusion statements taken from the National Curriculum in 2014 which should be borne in mind when considering individuals needs within the school's curriculum intent are the following:

• High expectations for every pupil
• Stretching work for pupils whose attainment is significantly above the expected standard, for pupils who have low levels of prior attainment or come from disadvantaged backgrounds
• Overcome potential barriers for individuals and groups of pupils
• Ensure no bias according to race, disability, sex, religion or belief, sexual orientation, pregnancy and maternity and gender reassignment
• No barriers to every pupil achieving
• Take account of the needs of pupils whose first language is not English

I discussed in Chapter 1 how 'curriculum' does not mean solely 'National Curriculum' and the freedoms we as practitioners have within the entire school curriculum. There are certain freedoms even within the National Curriculum with regard to sequencing as stated in the document itself:

> The key stage 2 programmes of study for English, mathematics and science are presented in this document as 'lower' (years 3 and 4) and 'upper' (years 5 and 6). This distinction is made as guidance for teachers and is not reflected in legislation. **The legal requirement is to cover the content of the programmes of study for years 3 to 6 by the end of key stage 2**.
>
> (DfE 2013)

With these freedoms in mind, I wanted to change the culture of teaching from 'working through the objectives' to 'inspiring others.' When I lead the first phase of our curriculum development I asked staff to consider what was meant by the term *curriculum* as we have explored in Chapter 1 and evaluate what was working well with our current school curriculum as well as what needed to change. I then introduced a card-sorting activity to explore some common myths about restrictions and freedoms where staff had to sort statements into piles of 'sometimes', 'never' and 'always' according to how much freedom we have. Through this we highlighted key freedoms as illustrated in the document: *Excellence and Enjoyment – A Strategy for Primary Schools* (Clarke 2003). Although this is an old document, these freedoms remain. For example, schools are free to decide how to teach, which aspects of a subject pupils will study in depth and how long to spend on a subject (this was a common misconception that specific time allocations must be adhered to for example 5 hours of maths and English per week and at least 2 hours of science); however, this is not the case, and whilst some guidance had been published by the Qualifications and Curriculum Authority, as I have mentioned earlier on, it is guidance and not law. In addition, schools are free to decide how to arrange learning during the school day; there is no requirement for subjects to be taught discretely. Once we overcame these hurdles, the staff felt liberated from perceived limitations and inspired to make change happen.

The next task was to consider our school curriculum through three lenses: 'Purpose, Opportunities and Balance'. I shall explore these in more detail next.

I asked staff to examine the 'purpose' from a child's perspective: 'Why am I doing this?' 'What are we working towards?' and 'Why does it matter to me?.' I suppose some of this was due to my own frustrations as a learner, particularly in secondary maths when I used to regularly ask my maths teacher, 'Why are we learning this?' her reply would often be 'For fun!' As a team we drew up a list of what we felt was important for our children and what we wanted our school curriculum to achieve. This was then used as a curriculum audit throughout the process of change (see Table 7.1).

After considering the purpose of what we were proposing to teach, I wanted us to consider the types of opportunities we were providing to our learners in order to develop as successful learners, confident individuals and responsible citizens; to gain new knowledge and skills; to acquire core subject skills; to apply these in exciting contexts; and to develop and apply essential skills and attitudes to enhance positive learning and life experiences. We discussed a thematic curriculum, sometimes referred to as a 'creative curriculum', which was our preferred term, through which subjects are connected by a theme as well as wider opportunities such as working with other

*Table 7.1* Table of requirements identified by staff for a high quality curriculum

| **Does our curriculum:** | *Rarely* | *Mostly* | *Always* |
|---|---|---|---|
| Deliver contextualised learning relevant to our children at appropriate age levels for enjoyment and engagement/motivated learners, responding to children's own interest | | | |
| Give students confidence and opportunities for success | | | |
| Give the learners ownership, instilling positive attitudes to learning | | | |
| Provide opportunities to reflect on learning | | | |
| Develop independent, creative flexible learners | | | |
| Enable the application of skills and knowledge | | | |
| Provide flexibility in terms of timetable – time to become absorbed in an activity | | | |
| Have structure and develop key skills and knowledge in English, maths, computing science | | | |
| Incorporate discrete skills in other subject areas such as history; geography; Personal, Social, Health and Economic education; etc. | | | |
| Challenge expectations and sharing these with children | | | |
| Offer children useful feedback and engage them actively in the learning process | | | |
| Explore prior knowledge and build on this | | | |
| Use a wide repertoire of teaching and learning approaches matching strategies to contexts and needs | | | |
| Build on a good understanding of child development | | | |

Audit tool to examine current approach to curriculum against agreed ideals agencies. Different ways of working were suggested to give pupils more independence; some of these, such as 'Mantle of the Expert', are discussed in Chapter 8.

Next, we had to ensure we were providing variety and balance across all curriculum areas. Variety is the spice of life, and as we have already concluded, we cannot accurately predict the skills each pupil will need for their future, so it is essential to provide a smorgasbord for children to develop a wide range of skills and acquire a broad knowledge base. It was important when discussing themes that we balanced them throughout the year so that if one was biased towards science, then others were more humanities-based for example. We also decided that maths and English would be taught daily and that there would be cross-curricular opportunities provided for the application of skills. As the curriculum leader, I was clear that some subjects could lie 'fallow' for a period so long as they were picked up throughout the school year. This allowed for greater flexibility, more cohesion within the topic and fewer tenuous links. I monitored this by taking in long-term plans from each year group in which National Curriculum objectives and wider experiences for each year group had been colour coded by staff to show in which term they had been taught. The staff had the flexibility to be creative and teach in a thematic way, and I had an overview of the objectives taught for each subject to know that we had covered the National Curriculum as a minimum.

Ofsted (2018) summarised that a 'high-quality curriculum:

- Is based on proactive thinking
- Will be the product or clear consideration of the sequence of content necessary for children to make progress
- Will provide children with the knowledge they need for subsequent learning— transferable knowledge
- Builds deeper understanding and the capacity for skilful performance'

In Chapter 8, I outline a range of approaches and methodologies which can be adopted or not. This will not be a detailed analysis as many books have been published and I am not advocating any singular approach, although I am keen to showcase a range of innovative and engaging options in order to inspire creativity and challenge preconceptions.

During my time as an Ofsted inspector, we examined the curriculum in each school to see that it met the needs of all: Did it support the needs of the children with

Special Education Needs and Disabilities (SEND)? Did it challenge the most able? Were boys or girls disadvantaged by it? Were those children who were identified as 'disadvantaged' given ample opportunities and support to make accelerated progress? Were any groups of vulnerable children left behind? These are the types of questions school leaders should be asking themselves when designing their curriculum:

> - Why are we teaching that, and why in the order we have chosen?
> - Is there a clear sequence of learning to support future learning and eventually employment?
> - Do any vulnerable groups have the potential to be left behind?
> - Does the curriculum meet the needs of all learners so that they may succeed in life?
> - Are ambitions high for all groups of learners, in particular those with SEND or who are disadvantaged?
> - Is the curriculum 'broad and balanced'? Does it include a wide range of skills and learning opportunities under a variety of disciplines?

This book was conceived through my love of teaching, my passion for creativity and my desire to share with a wider audience the freedoms that we have as teachers, celebrating some of the most engaging ideas which have been implemented with real classes of children. My fear is that some school leaders and teachers feel they should be 'Ofsted ready' and use phrases such as 'Ofsted would like this', which leads to perceived limitations on freedom. Ofsted has gone a long way to try to dispel myths about 'what Ofsted want', and in fact, my own recent experiences as an inspector opened my eyes even more to this. The keys to a positive Ofsted grade are knowing your school well, being aware of and meeting all children's needs and ensuring that all children make progress. Surely this is what every school leader wants regardless of an external audit, although I acknowledge it is gratifying to have it recognised when it is going well and useful to have it highlighted when it is not.

I am delighted that there is a greater focus by inspectors on the educational diet provided to children though I am also wary that schools will look for an 'outstanding curriculum'. In my experience of curriculum development, there are many peddlers of such an 'off the peg' curriculum, and each has its own merits; however, I return to my point about the children's needs and their passions which should be embraced. I also refer to my training as an inspector during which it was drilled into us that there Ofsted does not have a 'preferred method', that is to say, that there is no one right way to do things, no singular 'outstanding curriculum' to follow. The National Curriculum 2014 provides 'an outline of core knowledge around which teachers can develop **exciting and stimulating lessons** to promote the development of pupils' knowledge, understanding and skills as part of the wider school curriculum' (emphasis added). It is these exciting and stimulating lessons to which this next section of Chapter 7 is dedicated.

## Implementation

So now we turn to 'implementation'. *Implementation* means 'what is actually taught in the classroom'; straight away there is freedom in this statement; we have the freedom to define what we mean by 'classroom' as it does not have to be inside four walls. This could quite easily be an outdoor classroom, such as a seated area with open sides and a roof, a wooded area such as within a Forest School or even a virtual classroom online, teaching simultaneously in different homes, as was the case for many including myself during the COVID-19 pandemic from March 2020 for five months and again from January 2021. In this section there are lots of practical ideas for the busy teacher. Many thanks go to my friends/colleagues/contributors for providing me with a wealth of ideas that you have put into practice in your own classrooms. These fun and engaging activity ideas and lesson outlines can be adapted to a variety of themes and subjects.

How exciting to immerse the children in the experience and the world of imagination. It is clear to see in an excellent example shown in Table 7.2 of how a simple theme can lead to cross-curricular learning; in Early Years, this is known as 'continuous provision' so that children can access tasks linked to the main theme throughout the week. These activities would be available for children to explore as a mixture of child-led and adult-led tasks. For a similar theme in Key Stage 1 or 2, this would be linked to other subjects but would work in the same way. In providing the children with this exciting stimulus of the 'CCTV' (closed-circuit television) footage we are immersing them in the problem and inviting them to find different solutions to looking after an egg whilst also encouraging them to make marks for communication purposes linked to their own ideas and exploration on caring for the dinosaur egg. Take time to look back at Chapter 1 to see how this example brilliantly illustrates the practitioner's role in developing creative thinkers.

Table 7.2 Early Years activity

| | |
|---|---|
| **Subject and age range:** | *Early Years Foundation Stage (EYFS) – Communication and language (listening) and Literacy (writing).* |
| **National Curriculum/ Early Years objective/ aim of lesson:** | Children listen attentively in a range of situations. They listen to stories, accurately anticipating key events and respond to what they hear with relevant comments, questions, or actions. They give their attention to what others say and respond appropriately while engaged in another activity. |
| | Children use their phonic knowledge to write words in ways which match their spoken sounds. They also write some irregular common words. They write simple sentences which can be read by themselves and others. Some words are spelt correctly, and others are phonetically plausible. |
| **Context:** | This was a sequence of lessons I observed while undertaking my teaching practice, within a topic of dinosaurs. |
| | The teacher had delivered a lesson on eggs and what they need to hatch (understanding the world). |
| | The class teacher made a video of the classroom and used the Monster Park app (available for free) to add an animation of a dinosaur into the classroom. The children found an egg in a box in the classroom along with a letter (explaining that the mother dinosaur has left her egg for the children to look after and that they needed to be very careful with the egg so they had to think of ways they could look after it (links to Personal Social and Emotional Development (PSED). Children were shown the video of the dinosaur in the classroom as if it were on closed-circuit television (CCTV). The adult asked the children what we could write back to the dinosaur then modelled this. As an adult-led task, children were to write a message back to the mother dinosaur. |
| **What was the impact? What more did the pupils know and/or could do?** | The children were very engaged and excited by the thought of a dinosaur in their classroom, demonstrating the characteristics of effective learning during free flow around dinosaurs and the egg. The use of the video and the element of surprise motivated children who for example sometimes struggle with listening while sitting on the carpet. |
| | During the adult-led task, children practised writing for the purpose ascribing meaning to marks they make (30–50 months), working towards their own targets to develop their writing with guidance from the adult. |
| **Any other notes:**<br><br>**Continuous provision ideas:** | Observing a hatching egg (such as the ones you put in water and they hatch) with magnifying glasses (understanding the world, the world.) Early learning goal: Children know about similarities and differences in relation to places, objects, materials and living things. They talk about the features of their own immediate environment and how environments might vary from one another. They make observations of animals and plants and explain why some things occur and talk about changes. |
| | Making nests for the egg (expressive arts and design, exploring and using media and materials). |

*(Continued)*

*Table 7.2* (Continued)

| **Subject and age range:** | *Early Years Foundation Stage (EYFS) – Communication and language (listening) and Literacy (writing).* |
|---|---|
| | Dinosaurs frozen in balloons (understanding the world: the world (40–60 months), looks closely at similarities, differences, patterns, and change). |
| | Dinosaur excavation in a tuff tray (such as the ones that you can buy, I made these relatively cheaply by using 1 part sand, 1 cup plaster of Paris, 1/2 to 3/4 cup of water (more if needed) and dinosaur toys and rocks, and pouring the mixture into disposable containers, away from the children while making). The children then enjoyed scraping out the mixture using cuticle sticks and any safe scraping tools to see what they could find inside. (Physical development: moving and handling [40–60 months]; Uses simple tools to effect changes to materials; Handles tools, objects, construction, and malleable materials safely and with increasing control). |
| | How many dinosaur stomps/jumps/roars/tail swishes can you do in 30 seconds? (Mathematics, Shape space measure [40–60 months], Measures short periods of time in simple ways). |
| | Taking care of hard-boiled eggs in sand- boiled in water and food colouring (PSED: managing feelings and behaviour, aware of own feelings, and knows that some actions and words can hurt others' feelings [30–50 months]). |

The next lesson, shown in Table 7.3, was an experience which started as a small idea to create music using car parts to link music with our theme of 'vehicles'. First of all, I needed to acquire the 'instruments'. Due to our location on the border of Northamptonshire and Oxfordshire, I contacted a local F1 team to see if it was possible to use some car parts from an F1 car; however, due to creative licences, this was not possible. However, I looked at other options and made contact with BMW Mini which was also close to our school. After many meetings, legal documents and much generosity on the part of the people I was working with, we received a delivery of clean car parts; some were even mounted to make them easier to use as instruments. These were delivered in a Mini car, and the children were lucky enough to have a tour around the vehicle so that they could identify each car part which was going to be used in a very different way once it was in their hands. This was a unique project for all of us, and you may not be lucky enough to have the same positive response from a car manufacturer that we received; however, why limit this to car parts and who is to say that it would make sense to your project. Perhaps garden equipment might be a better fit or instruments from a particular country you are studying would be appropriate.

*Table 7.3* Year 3 music activity

| Subject and age range: | Music (Year 3 class) |
|---|---|
| National Curriculum objective/aim of lesson: | KS2: They should develop an understanding of musical composition, organising and manipulating ideas within musical structures and reproducing sounds from aural memory.<br><br>… appreciate and understand a wide range of high-quality live and recorded music drawn from different traditions and from great composers and musicians |
| Context: | This was a series of lessons set in the context of the learning topic 'Vehicles.' I had a crazy idea to create an orchestra from car parts as a way of incorporating music into our theme. This project grew and incorporated BMW Oxford and Oxford University professors.<br><br>BMW Oxford generously donated car parts to the cause and even brought cars to the school so the children could see their 'instruments' in their original locations. Following this, in conjunction with the music faculty at Oxford University, the children were exposed to live Indonesian Gamelan music which they later emulated on car parts and performed at the centenary celebrations of BMW Oxford. In addition to this, children created sounds which were recorded and edited using electronics to enhance and distort the sounds, morphing them from one pure sound to another previously unheard creation. |
| What was the impact? What more did the pupils know and/or could do? | • Children were aware of world music which they had previously not been exposed to.<br>• They had the opportunity to work with professors from the university and explore the musical quality of car parts.<br>• They were able to play together as an orchestra using cohesive rhythm and a musical pattern.<br>• Children's confidence was boosted as they performed to a large audience in a public space. |
| Any other notes: | This could easily be replicated with kitchen utensils, or items found in a bathroom, or more generally around the house/classroom. It need not be Indonesian gamelan as the stimulus but any another style of music. |

I was concerned with my level of musical expertise in making this dream happen, so I decided to reach out to Oxford University, which was local to my school, and ask if anyone was willing to be involved in such a project. I could not have imagined the fantastic response which led to the children experiencing Indonesian gamelan music with huge traditional instruments filling the hall and my class of 8-year-olds being taught by professors from Oxford University and later applying their learning to a creative interpretation of rhythms and sounds on the car parts from the music they had heard and the rhythms they had created using their hands to clap and tap. In addition to this, we explored ways to distort and alter sounds electronically as led by a doctoral student. Another professor guided the children in creating a variety of different sounds and rhythms using the car parts we had been generously donated by BMW Mini, also based in Oxford. It was a coincidence that our school project coincided with the 100-year anniversary of BMW Mini, and we were invited as special guests to play at their Family Celebration Day. What a fantastic culmination of our work. In addition to this, the team at Oxford University created a theatrical musical presentation of 'Vehicles' and our recordings were also featured in this. The key message here is that reaching out to other organisations can be a great way to enhance the curriculum provision at your school and can take you beyond your wildest dreams.

The following lesson, detailed in Table 7.4, took a bit of preparation in terms of grating chocolate; I would highly recommend an electric grater on a food processor for speed. If you have a school kitchen, they may be able to help here or a kind parent perhaps. Safety, hygiene and allergies must be a high priority given that the end product can be eaten. This activity is great fun for the children, enhances the need to carefully listen to instructions and beautifully demonstrates the rock cycle (Table 7.4).

What a brilliantly open theme of 'The Sky' in this next example and fantastic opportunities for children to really engage with their learning and drive it forward themselves (no pun intended!). In the activity detailed in Table 7.5, it is clear how motivated the children were when they were so involved in the purpose of their learning, a real-life problem which the children identified and solved for themselves. The open 'theme' lent itself to flexibility and creativity, but this also required openness on the part of the teacher to enable the children to follow their interests. I am a huge fan of community involvement, (ensuring safeguarding is paramount of course). It was great to see children educating their parents and working with the local council and business to seek permission for and produce the poster. This is writing for a reason and the teacher reported a high level of engagement from the children as it had ignited a passion in them, and there was a clear requirement to persuade others of their cause (Table 7.5).

The activity shown in Table 7.6 is an excellent example of creativity in that it starts with an abstract example of 'pairing' or 'words which go together', making links between the marriage of words and the marriage of people. Open questions challenge the learners to justify their reasoning when providing possible answers to

*Table 7.4* Year 3 science activity

| **Subject and age range:** | *Science (Year 3 class)* |
|---|---|
| **National Curriculum objective/aim of lesson:** | KS2: compare and group together different kinds of rocks on the basis of their appearance and simple physical properties.<br><br>To make a chocolate rock and explore the rock cycle, noting different properties. |
| **Context:** | Within the context of learning about rocks from first-hand observations, this in itself is a one-off lesson.<br><br>Children are provided with a plastic cup, clingfilm, grated milk and white chocolate and spoons. Children then line their cup with clingfilm, put 5 teaspoons of grated milk chocolate in the cup, and then add 5 teaspoons of white chocolate on top and then a further 5 tsp of milk chocolate. They then apply pressure and time to the 'sediment' (encourage them to push down quite hard but beware of doing this in hot weather!). They need to do this for approximately 5 minutes applying pressure evenly over the chocolate 'sediment' so that it cements together. Carefully lift it out and break in half, you should be able to see 'layers' in the sedimentary rock.<br><br>With the other half, children mould it into a ball in their hands (still wrapped in clingfilm); this melts the outside of the rock and represents more time, pressure and heat. Cut this open to show how the outside has changed, but deep in the core, the sedimentary layers can still be seen. Whilst some won't show this clearly you should get a good sample [5–10] in a class of 30 which shows this really well. For the igneous rock, I demonstrate this using a mug of hot water and my demonstrated version of the metamorphic rock. I dunk it in the hot water … still in clingfilm then pop it in the fridge (overnight). The following day I cut this in half to show the children the greater change on the outside of the rock and the 'marbling' on the inside. |
| **What was the impact? What more did the pupils know and/or could do?** | • Children were fully engaged since they could eat the 'experiment'.<br>• They experienced the rock cycle and understood how rocks change over time with heat and pressure.<br>• When they sang a song about the rock cycle, they could 'see' each stage in their heads by recollecting the experiment. |
| **Any other notes** | Ensuring health and safety is a high priority at all times; letters should be sent home to ensure there are no allergies; children can still make it even if they can't eat it so long as the allergic reaction is only to ingestion.<br><br>Children must wash their hands before handling chocolate and surfaces must be wiped clean with an appropriate sanitizer too.<br><br>I have also seen biscuits and thick icing/frosting used effectively to demonstrate the movement of tectonic plates in geography when exploring mountain ridges and volcano formations. |

*Table 7.5* Year 5 science/stewardship activity

| | |
|---|---|
| **Subject**: | *Stewardship – caring for our world.*<br>Year 5 'The Sky.' |
| **National Curriculum objective/ aim of lesson**: | The children were asked to brainstorm and think of their own ideas and come up with their own questions that they wanted to explore.<br><br>From this, our science was based on the question: what is beyond the sky? How do we know? This included stories and beliefs from religions and history. Then we covered the Year 5 science Space curriculum. We also learned about air resistance and they were fascinated with aeroplanes. This led us to read a great book about the Wright brothers, and they enjoyed this so much we used it as our main literacy focus. |
| **Context**: | This was a series of lessons around the theme, and children drove their own learning forward.<br><br>They wanted to find out what is in the air (apart from the gases it is made from). For a science experiment, they hung sticky paper in different areas inside and outside the school building. The results showed more pollution stuck to the paper near the road next to the school where parents drop off and pick up. This led to lots of research and discussions about what pollution might be in the air and where it came from.<br><br>The children were shocked to discover what car exhaust fumes actually contain, the harm they can cause their growing bodies and we discovered that the law says it's illegal to idle – keeping the car engine running while stationary and parked on a public road for more than 30 seconds. The children were excited and enraged by this new information (some 'snitched' on their parents there and then!), and they went home that night and 'educated' their parents – many parents told me the next day that they had been told off by their child for doing this when waiting for someone. One child even timed her mum that evening and told her to switch her engine off at 30 seconds! The parent obliged as she said her daughter made her feel guilty.<br><br>One boy said there are other parents who do not know the damaging effects car fumes have on our health. Buses, tractors, lorries and other villagers also use the road and stop to chat to someone with the engine running is wrong. He suggested a large banner would be a good idea to let the people driving through the village know to turn their engines off when stopped. The rest of the class agreed it was a good idea. So we asked a member of the village council who we needed to ask to get permission to put such a large sign outside our school for motorists to see. He said the village council would make the decision if they understood why it was necessary.<br><br>That led to letters being planned, drafted and sent to the council and to our headteacher requesting permission. The children wrote about their findings from the science experiment, the information from the research they carried out and their determination to make the air cleaner outside our school so that the children attending would all remain healthy. They were driven and motivated, and they were some of the best letters I have ever read from children after teaching for over 20 years. They had a real purpose to them and the children were buzzing. |

*(Continued)*

*Table 7.5* (Continued)

| | |
|---|---|
| **Subject**: | *Stewardship – caring for our world.*<br>*Year 5 'The Sky.'* |
| | A member of the village council then came into the school to thank the children for their letters and to ask them some more questions. He concluded his visit by saying he was convinced that the children's arguments for a banner justified the need for one. He told the class the whole council were impressed with their letters, and they could see how strongly they felt. He then said the council would give the children £100 to have a professional banner made. |
| | So then to art, design and computing. The children spent several lessons on this. First, they had to decide on what to include – not too many words but enough to get the point across – something eye-catching and bright and no copying icons from the internet that had a copyright. They sketched ideas and drew pictures. They searched for ideas on the net and used iPads to design our banner using a graphics program. The finished design only took a few days to make using a local design company. |
| | The children then wanted to find out what else pollutes our skies. This led to more research in small groups, presentations made, parents were invited into our class and the children all presented their findings. They included the history of aviation and why planes pollute our skies today, how clothes manufacturing contributes to air pollution, choosing to buy local foods and to look at packaging to be more conscious of air miles travelled by the food on our tables and so on. They told their parents about the process we went through from start to finish to explain why the banner is there. We then went outside and unveiled the banner with our parents. It is still there today, and we plan to move it to different locations near our school to make more people notice it. |
| **What was the impact? What more did the pupils know and/or could do?** | The aim of our school curriculum is to learn about things that are purposeful. Although I had already planned the direction in which to take the theme, the children helped in deciding their own learning. We want children to understand their own importance and to know they can make a difference. We want the children to become good stewards – ones who care about our world, the people in it and its future. We want them to become good citizens, motivated learners, to feel valued, to be good ambassadors for worthy causes and to be courageous advocates. |
| **Any other notes** | We arrange our curriculum around themes: caring for our world, caring for the people in our world and caring for ourselves. Through these we can include a range of learning from the whole curriculum. We want our children to be inspired and leave school understanding how their learning can help them in their own futures. |

the suggestions posed. It is multicultural in its approach with an extension task of exploring and gathering facts about marriages in a range of cultures and religions, which, given the school make-up is no surprise, but even in a homogeneous village school of predominantly white pupils (for example), this multicultural approach is important for fostering open minds and preparing children to be active citizens in

*Table 7.6* Year 5 PSHE activity

| Subject: | PSHE – Marriage and Relationships |
|---|---|
| **National Curriculum objective/ aim of lesson**: | To understand what makes a good and healthy relationship<br><br>Success criteria:<br>• I must be able to talk about different types of relationships.<br>• I should be able to recognise what a healthy relationship consists of and what it might look like.<br>• I could explain why people choose to make the commitment of marriage/ civil ceremonies and what the law says about it. |
| **Context**: | First lesson in a series based on marriage and relationships. Year 5 class in a particularly multicultural school in the suburbs of Leicester. Spring term. Pupils were given the opportunity to learn about and reflect upon the following given objectives given:<br><br>R5. that civil partnerships and marriage are examples of a public demonstration of the commitment made between two people who love and care for each other and want to spend their lives together and who are of the legal age to make that commitment<br><br>R19. that two people who love and care for one another can be in a committed relationship and not be married or in a civil partnership<br><br>R20. that forcing anyone to marry is a crime; that support is available to protect and prevent people from being forced into marriage and to know how to get support for themselves or others |
| **What was the impact? What more did the pupils know and/or could do?** | ALL children could access the lesson without additional resources, all opinions were valid and academic ability wasn't a factor. It evoked opinions and debates which I hadn't even considered when planning the lesson as well as poetic and imaginative flair at the start of the session, when the children were asked to think of two-word love stories:<br><br>Hot chocolate, Chocolate orange, Clean sheets, Hot bath, comfy slippers, Smooth pebble, Hand-knitted<br><br>They didn't want to stop this warm-up activity as they became so engrossed in objects they love involving two words.<br><br>Children were presented with a number of scenarios in which they had to discuss whether they were positive or negative and most crucially why they thought this. The debate which took me by surprise was when answering the following questions:<br>• **My dad doesn't like my mum going out**.<br>Positive or Negative? Why?<br>• **My mum told my brother he wasn't allowed to see his friends for a week because he got into trouble at school**.<br>Positive or Negative? Why?<br><br>They debated the issues surrounding why the dad's behaviour might be controlling or caring and then the issue surrounding being grounded. Later in the session, a girl in my class who is usually very quiet became quite animated when talking about her own experience of her parent's marriage and divorce in the family. This 10-year-old girl doesn't usually contribute anything in class discussions, so I was very pleasantly surprised to hear her speak out. |

modern Britain. In a school with children from a variety of backgrounds, it ensures the lesson is in a context familiar to them and the inclusion of celebrities makes sure that children who do not have an immediate experience of weddings within their own family also have a resource to draw on. The lesson also studied the legal aspects of marriage helping children to understand the rule of law in context. Children were then invited to reflect on 'successful marriages' they knew about; this could be from their own families, friends or celebrities. Their final task was to draw up a list of top 10 criteria for a happy and lasting marriage. This task required convergent thinking in pulling together all the thoughts they had evaluated and facts they had learnt, assimilating it into a single short document.

## Impact

To quote Ofsted (2019), '[t]he end result of a good, well-taught curriculum is that pupils know more and are able to do more'. In other words, the positive results of pupils' learning can then be seen in the standards they achieve. How do you know what the impact of teaching is on pupil outcomes if you do not observe, measure or assess it?

In the last few years, however, assessment has wrongly been at the forefront of learning; there has been a focus on the end results and targets for children to achieve a particular milestone, I have even been asked by a headteacher to 'perform miracles' in order to achieve targets for the number of children achieving a particular level of attainment. Many schools run revision classes for Year 6 children in the holidays and after school. This extends to secondary schools also but is not the scope of this book. There is certainly a top-down pressure on Year 6 teachers in many schools to ensure children reach their targets. Indeed, children should be enabled to make progress, reach targets and also enjoy learning; however, the focus on numbers has led to a 'teach to the test' culture where the curriculum has been narrowed in order to focus on revision, past papers and examination skills. Ofsted's chief inspector, Amanda Spielman (2017), discusses findings from research into the curriculum and states:

> 'It seems unlikely that any school has prioritised testing over the curriculum as a deliberate choice.' She acknowledges that '[i]nspection may well have unintentionally contributed to the shift by reinforcing the focus on measures' and crucially highlights 'that any test can only ever sample the knowledge that has been gained.'

This is a pivotal step in helping schools to identify that a rich and varied curriculum leads to positive outcomes rather than focusing on the outcomes and narrowing the curriculum as we have already examined in Chapter 4.

Assessment is naturally part of the learning cycle: plan, do, review. Throughout the process of teaching and learning, teachers are continually assessing what the learners have understood; this can take many forms but is usually informal. It can be through observations, conversations with the child, working alongside them and written feedback. This enables the teacher to identify gaps in learning or misconceptions so that these can be addressed either immediately, at the end of the lesson or in a follow-up lesson depending on the size of the gap in learning or misconception and the time available.

Self-assessment is a very useful tool; children can show with their hands or coloured cards their level of understanding (e.g. green for 'I've got this', amber for 'I'm getting there but need more practice' and red for 'I really need more help!'). With practice and guidance, children can identify their own errors. Peer assessment is also helpful here; children can even help each other to develop their understanding, but this should be monitored by an adult to ensure both parties have correctly understood the concept. Where this is done well, with the use of success criteria and clear examples and where children have developed their ability to be objective, it can have a huge positive impact for both children in terms of self-esteem and securing knowledge.

On an educational visit to Finland in 2016, I saw much that inspired me, including a maths lesson in which children had to hunt for answers around the school. I have repeated this with multiplication tables in a Year 3 class, and a friend who was homeschooling also used the idea with her energetic daughter. She was given the questions and had to locate the answers; this could also be reversed by giving children the answer and asking them to find the question or a mixture of both! However, something else which I was keen to replicate on my return was the use of technology for formative assessments. Some classes used Kahoot, which is not solely used in Finland; however, it was not something I had experienced in the UK. It consists of a series of quiz questions set up by the teacher to assess learners' knowledge of a topic. Children log in to the quiz on their own mobile devices, in most cases their mobile phone; questions are projected onto a large screen, with corresponding colours and symbols sent to their devices to select an answer from multiple choices. The challenge I faced on return to a primary school classroom is the 1:1 access to a mobile device is non-existent in the school

I worked in and for many other schools. 'Bring your own device', especially mobile phones, is not encouraged mainly due to safeguarding reasons, so if for any reason children do bring these into school, they are usually locked away in the school office. Whilst visiting a primary school in the UK, I discovered 'Plickers'. This offered me the perfect alternative, the concept of a multiple-choice quiz was at the heart, and I could design a bank of quizzes from home on a website with up to four options per question; these could include images or text as answers. The images came in especially handy when I wanted to set quiz questions on maths shapes or items for telling time. The particular benefit of 'Plickers' was that children did not need a device. A QR code card like the one shown in Figure 7.1 is assigned to each child; each card is numbered and can be assigned to an individual, and the orientation of the card allows for four multiple-choice answers: A, B, C or D.

There are only a few disadvantages to this in that it relies on a fully charged and working digital device to read the card and another to show the questions such as a computer and a large screen. There are, however, many advantages to using this type of technology in place of a 'show of hands'. First of all, it is much more fun and engaging for the learners concerned (I always had a 'guest' card so that any visitors to the classroom could participate as well!). With a hands-up approach, you get a general overview, but it is more of a challenge to identify quickly the names

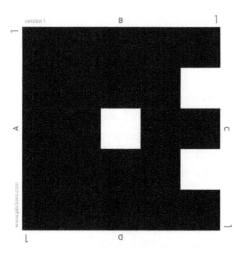

Figure 7.1: A QR code for use with a formative assessment platform called Plickers

of children who were unsure, and often they are embarrassed to identify themselves. With 'Plickers', the teacher quickly scans the cards held up by the children and it will register each response. I was impressed by how quick and efficient this was, scanning as though taking a panoramic photograph would pick up all but a few cards, making it easy to identify any children who had not responded; once all have responded, there is a facility to publicly share the graph of answers without names and to highlight the correct answer (if you set this up when inputting the questions), which always generated a cheer from those who had answered correctly. In addition to this, on the scanning device, the names of children who gave the incorrect answer are flagged up; they can be monitored over a series of questions to note a pattern or a one-off error. These data are also stored on the website so can be accessed later via any device. This can then inform future planning and additional support for those who need it. In Figure 7.2, an example analysis of one question, with those having the correct answer highlighted in green, is shown.

## Which fraction is the largest?                ● 68%

● Year 3

Thursday 24 May 2018 9:56 AM                                              ...

| A | 6/16 | | | | 17 |
|---|------|--|--|--|----|

| Adam | Darcey | Kian | Sophie |
|------|--------|------|--------|
| Aiden | Emily | Kyra | Vin |
| Alfie | Evie | Leo | |
| Ben | Henry | Leon | |
| Charlie | Joe | Mason | |

| B | 2/8 | 1 |
|---|-----|---|

Jasmine

| C | 1/4 | 7 |
|---|-----|---|

| Asha | Meredith | Rebecca | Seth |
|------|----------|---------|------|
| Keith | Nyah | Sam | |

D                                                                        0

Missing                                                                  4

| Kayden | Niall |
|--------|-------|
| Leah | 30 Guest |

Figure 7.2: An image from Plickers identifying children who answered the question correctly and those who did not

This type of assessment is commonly known as 'formative' assessment. I remember the term as it is 'informative', a useful snapshot of information to pinpoint any individuals or groups who need some extra teaching to fully understand the concept being taught. At the end of the unit or the year comes a 'summative' assessment, which shows how well children have retained the information and skills. Or as Ofsted (2019) phrases it, '[h]ow well are children learning the content outlined in the curriculum?' Something can only be remembered if it is truly understood; if a fact or a skill is not understood, there is nothing succinct to remember. It is clear to see then how the two types of assessment go hand-in-hand, without formative assessment of any kind there is no way to identify errors and correct them. Once a formative assessment has been carried out and support put in place, children are more likely to understand and retain what they have learnt which will be evident in summative assessments.

It is also important to track a child's progress over time and with that in mind I introduced 'Pupil Progress Meetings'. These meetings were held termly with myself and the class teacher looking at the assessment data from their class. It is stating the obvious to say that it isn't enough to just input data; it is the analysis and actions arising from it are the crucial part. These meetings evolved over time but essentially tracked children from Early Years to the end of Key Stage 1 and from the end of Key Stage 1 to end of Key Stage 2, exploring their journey along the way. It was important to identify those children who were on track to meet their Early Learning Goals as soon as possible and also those who may have fallen short requiring intervention in a particular area such as behaviour or speech and language. It was also interesting to identify those children who were very confident and hitting the Early Learning Goals before the end of Reception who therefore required further challenge to keep them inspired and learning. For each year group above Reception, this pattern continued, and it was intriguing to challenge perceptions about those children who were achieving in line with national expectations for their age, but perhaps some of these children had achieved above expectations in previous years, so although on first glance the data look promising, these children are, in fact, underachieving as they are capable of more. Equally if children were achieving at age-related expectations (AREs) nationally in a particular year group but had previously been achieving below AREs, then they have made promising progress. It is important to explore groups by previous achievement at key stages, gender, ethnicity, term of birth, Special Educational Needs and Disabilities, free school meals and any other groups pertinent to the school circumstances. The reason for this is to identify if there are school-wide issues which need addressing rather than specifically for individual pupils. This approach can highlight a need to change a particular intervention if it identifies a lack of positive impact.

The statement at the start of this section on Impact, clearly sits summative assessment in its rightful place; at the end of a teaching sequence. Pupils learn because of high-quality teaching and an exciting curriculum offer; assessment should merely measure the effectiveness of this. However, assessment in terms of analysing data and identifying trends should be seen as an activity which happens more frequently than annually as there is little which can be done at this point if a child has made poor progress in the year, whereas if identified earlier in the year, there is time to make a difference. Amanda Spielman (2017) summarises my thoughts when she says that 'good examination results … don't always mean that the pupil received rich and full knowledge from the curriculum'.

Cramming for tests is futile. It may achieve the desired result of the child passing a test and contributing to the schools' overall assessment information (data). However, if the curriculum intent is broader than this, aimed at developing well-rounded individuals and preparing them for their next step in education and as citizens of modern Britain, you could hardly declare that passing a test by intensive revision of skills and knowledge in specific curriculum areas was having the intended impact.

---

- How, when and why do we carry out formative assessment?
- What does it tell us?
- What do we do with the information? Does it feed into the current lesson or future planning, or is it carried out for the sake of it?
- How, when and why do we carry out summative assessment?
- What does it tell us? Are there any trends in particular groups?
- What do we do with the information? Do we use it to identify further staff training needs? Are interventions adapted, changed or applied more widely as a result?
- Do we need or want to change anything about our current practice?

## Bibliography

Journals and reports

Clarke, C. (2003) *Excellence and Enjoyment – A Strategy for Primary Schools* Available from: https://dera.ioe.ac.uk/4817/? Accessed 3 August 2021 April 2004.

DfE (2013) last updated 2015 *The National Curriculum in England: Key Stages 1 and 2 Framework Document* Available from: www.gov.uk/dfe/nationalcurriculum Accessed 3 June 2020.

Ofsted (2018) *An investigation into how to assess the quality of education through curriculum intent, implementation and impact* Online: Ofsted. Available from: https://assets.publishing.service.gov.uk/government/uploads/system/uploads/attachment_data/file/936097/Curriculum_research_How_to_assess_intent_and_implementation_of_curriculum_191218.pdf Accessed 3 June 2020.

Ofsted (2019) Inspecting the Curriculum. Available from: https://www.gov.uk/government/publications/inspecting-the-curriculum Accessed 26 November 2020.

Spielman, A. (2017) *HMCI's commentary: recent primary and secondary curriculum research*, London: Osfted. Available from: https://www.gov.uk/government/speeches/hmcis-commentary-october-2017 Accessed 10 March 2020.

Websites

https://help.plickers.com/hc/en-us/articles/360009395854-What-is-Plickers-

# Chapter 8

## A range of approaches

- What examples of 'curriculum' are on the market?
- What creative approaches to teaching and learning are there, and what does each have to offer?
- Examples of common themes and key principles from my research on our curriculum development journey and lessons I learned along the way

Hopefully after reading until this point you are inspired and ready to **implement** your own curriculum, you may be wondering if there is a need to or has someone already done the leg work. Is there an 'off the shelf/ready to go' school curriculum? In fact, there are many rich resources available to you, and at the start of my curriculum design journey, I visited many schools, attended seminars and carried out my own action research in school. It should be remembered that the National Curriculum is mandatory in maintained schools but not so for Free Schools or academies so long as a broad and balanced curriculum is provided as discussed earlier. In this chapter, I share some insights into a few of the options I studied. There is much more to be explored, and discovering a range of options led me to inspire our staff to create our own school curriculum with a combination of key elements from a range of approaches.

### International Primary Curriculum

The principle of the International Primary Curriculum (IPC) is to focus on a combination of academic, personal and international learning for children worldwide, combined with innovative and exciting ways to learn. In order to meet statutory requirements in England and Wales, this would need to be blended with the National Curriculum but has some great underlying principles and stimulating ideas.

The IPC is designed to help children

- learn the essential knowledge, skills and understanding of a broad range of curriculum subjects.
- engage with their learning so that they remain committed to learning throughout their school careers and their lives.
- develop the personal qualities they need to be good citizens and to respond to the changing contexts of their future lives.
- develop a sense of their own nationality and culture at the same time as developing a profound respect for the nationalities and cultures of others.

Key points I took away from this approach was that I wanted children to really engage with their learning and to develop the personal qualities to be good and active citizens, working together as a team as well as developing the resilience to work alone knowing when to ask for help and when to persevere alone.

## Learning Challenge Curriculum

At the start of my learning journey, I attended a conference on 'The Learning Challenge Curriculum' delivered by Clive Davies and others from Focus Education. There were some key points which stood out for me:

- A curriculum should be relevant to each school situation.
- It should challenge, excite and engage learners.
- It needs to develop higher-order thinking skills (to be fit for 21st century) which can be promoted through the use of questioning.
- Learning challenges are questions which stimulate and encourage discovery of an answer, these should be used rather than a 'Learning Objective' or 'WALT … We Are Learning To …' Rather than telling children what they will be learning, you are inviting them to explore the task with a question such as 'How can we …?' or 'Where do all the puddles go to?'
- Skills-based curriculum can be delivered via subjects or themes; there is no right or wrong.

Some subjects can lay 'fallow', in other words not taught at a particular point in time, but this needs to be monitored to make sure they are not missed altogether. When we planned our curriculum, some subjects and topic areas fit together more easily than others, and having the 'permission' (which we had previously perceived we needed) to teach subjects in blocks rather than all subjects throughout the year made the themed approach much easier and the links less contrived.

We chose a blended approach to a thematic and subject-based curriculum in that we continued to teach English, maths, French and physical education discreetly, although many skills learnt in these discreet lessons were applied to our theme which encompassed other subjects where the topic areas linked. Having previously planned on a document which was labelled in terms; for example in term 1, we will teach this area of science, and term 2 will be this topic; this was scrapped to plan in themes. In other words, so long as the long-term plan was covered within the year, it didn't matter (for the most part) which aspects were taught when. This is what I referred to in Chapter 5. The odd exception to this was if a particular topic in a subject was required to be taught as a prerequisite to another topic. A clear example of this is teaching multiplication and division in maths prior to teaching fractions.

## Mantle of the Expert

Mantle of the Expert involves the children taking on the responsibilities of people with expertise in an imaginary context. The core approach here is role-play. Children are aware of the realities of the classroom and of the 'make-believe' businesses they run; both the teacher and pupils dip in and out of this world of reality. Rather than talking to the class about the tasks we were about to undertake, I would call a 'business meeting' and explain that we had received an important phone call from a film company to make an educational video for primary school children about the 'Indus Valley' for example, for which the children, in groups, researched specific areas of knowledge and created their own short presentations, which they recorded on camera and were then put together as an entire film for the class to watch and learn about other areas of the Indus Valley. In another school we put on a real music festival, contacting bands and stall-holders, creating advertising banners and seeking out the best price for printing this in our given time scale as well as producing tickets and posters for the event. Some enterprises would lend themselves to real situations, involving others such as this one did, whilst some were more classroom and role-play-based. What they did all have in common was the element of fantasy and role-play, putting children in the role of the 'expert' making decisions. There was a clear purpose to the task, and cross-curricular learning was essential for success. One such 'enterprise' was 'SATs Busters', a Year 6 revision topic where children made their own games for Year 6 children to hone a particular maths skill. One child said: 'I was nervous about SATs [Standard Assessment Tests] before, then after our we ran our business I was excited and didn't realise we were revising.'

## The Black Curriculum

The Black Lives Matter movement has brought greater awareness of black history to the masses. For over 30 years, schools have paid attention to black history during Black History Month in October. The original aim was for the local community to challenge racism and educate themselves and others about the history that was not taught in schools. Our prime minister, Boris Johnson (2019), said,

> Black History Month always provides a fantastic opportunity for us to recognize the outstanding contributions people of African and Caribbean descent have made to our country over many generations.

This approach is rather outdated in terms of limiting the teaching of black history to one month of the year; you could say it is good that it is being acknowledged, but it does seem to be a rather token gesture. The Black Curriculum addresses concerns that 'currently, students across the UK are not being taught Black British History consistently as part of the national curriculum in a committed manner' and that 'Black history is not mandatory in schools which follow their own curriculum'. It also states very clearly that 'Black British history is not merely a theme for October but started hundreds of years before Windrush and pre-dates European colonial enslavement'. Its aim is to overcome these limitations by providing a curriculum for 365 days of the year!

## ProspectUs curriculum

The 'ProspectUs' curriculum is a bank of ideas and activities highlighting a variety of curriculum skills organised under themes for each year group. The documents set out clearly what knowledge and skills in each curriculum area are covered with links to the National Curriculum and identify 'fallow' subjects as I have highlighted in our approach too. Key questions under intent, implementation and impact in the overview of a unit encourage reflection about the purpose of teaching a particular theme and what opportunities are available to ensure children are engaged. There is a question to stimulate reflection about what children have learned rather than what activities they have participated in as well as identifying any outstanding gaps in understanding. It is very similar to the approach my school took, although we created ours ourselves and the advantage of this was that we were closely tracking the coverage of the National Curriculum through highlighting long-term plans and matching these to the learning coverage throughout the year. There would be no reason in my mind that this curriculum tracking approach could not be added to ensure essential skills are not omitted, and there is clear progression from Early Years to Year 6. The curriculum maps provided for each year identify the learning activities, so this could easily be linked to the National Curriculum or other curriculum learning objectives. This approach supports a blend of discrete skills teaching in the core subjects whilst also providing opportunities for the application of these skills within the context of the theme being studied. Practitioners are encouraged to celebrate the best examples of pupils' skills, through written work, displays throughout the school and shared drama productions and presentation assemblies.

## ABC does

For Early Years, objective-led planning Alistair Bryce Clegg advocates incorporating a learning objective into a child's play rather than interrupting their play to complete an adult-directed activity. Having identified the children's next steps, you can then ask questions relating to the objective whilst incorporating it into their play. For example, by asking questions such as 'I wonder how many pencils are in that pot?' whilst a child is drawing, you may find, as a fellow practitioner did, that the child could count beyond ten, add and subtract! This is especially useful for children who are reluctant to participate in an adult-directed activity.

## Forest School

Forest School is not just outdoor learning, which is also an invaluable element to the classroom; you only have to have worked with children for a few years or have your own children to be able to observe the difference in their behaviour when they are in an open space rather than within the same four walls. For many children, the fresh air and green spaces have an almost therapeutic effect. Forest School, however, is unique in that it is a long-term process of regular sessions, and the same process of planning, observing and adapting the next steps are reflected in standard classroom practice. Forest School 'supports the lifelong relationship between the learner and the natural world', and it is very learner-centred, much like the Montessori approach to learning, and encompasses 'being', 'doing' and 'learning'; the former of these is often unwittingly omitted in a classroom setting. It provides opportunities for learners to take supported risks and aims to foster 'resilient, confident. independent and creative learners'. Underpinning the Forest School principles as listed on its website, are some positive core beliefs, that learners are all

- equal, unique and valuable
- competent to explore & discover
- entitled to experience appropriate risk and challenge
- entitled to choose, and to initiate and drive their own learning and development
- entitled to experience regular success
- entitled to develop positive relationships with themselves and other people
- entitled to develop a strong, positive relationship with their natural world

## Philosophy for Children (P4C)

P4C encourages children to ask and discuss 'big questions' the types of questions where there is no single correct answer, such as 'Do we have to respect everyone?' or 'Is it okay to lie sometimes?' and where, as a 'community of enquiry', the group search for meaning together. In this context, it is perfectly okay to 'agree' or 'disagree' with someone else so long as you can give a reason. Philosophy therefore develops reasoning skills, critical thinking, analysing facts to form a judgement and making links between ideas. These skills are embedded in 'little c' creativity: creative thought. These skills require the ability to listen carefully to others and share their own views confidently yet have them challenged too and encourage reflection on original thoughts. In schools that have adopted P4C, I have observed children 'agreeing' or 'disagreeing' in constructive ways across the curriculum; it has become a part of their cultural norm. The 'I disagree with X because …' or 'My idea links with Y's …' discursive language is common in the classroom. P4C is a whole-school approach which can be used from the youngest to the oldest learners; it is incredible with the right support and opportunities how the youngest children can blow the minds of the facilitators with their thoughtful responses. I remember running a session with a Year 3 class who were incredibly thoughtful about a story they had heard in the media regarding turning off a very poorly baby's life support machine and they requested a P4C session to discuss it. I was worried they would be too upset by it and I told them so, but as a class, we took a vote that resulted in the session going ahead, and their thoughtful, caring responses amazed me.

At the end of the first year of research and planning, I asked all staff to ask their children what they had enjoyed in the year that was coming to an end and what they thought should change for next year's class. I collated this information, and there was much to digest. However, highlights which signalled the desire for change included a request to stay on a subject for longer and to not rush so much: 'not 4 weeks Romans, 4 weeks Tudors.' Children expressed a desire to choose their own subjects which we introduced the following year. Many children reported that drama helped their learning, saying it was fun and exciting. I think they liked the idea of role-play and being in a 'business' rather than a classroom. This supports the views of Vygotsky (1978), who stated that 'play creates a zone of proximal development of the child. In play a child always behaves beyond his average age, above his daily behaviour; in play it is as though he were a head taller than himself'. Children felt we should make more connections in our work and make the way we learn more 'fun'. I had been trialling the new approach with my Year 6 class, and their responses were very interesting when I surveyed them; they enjoyed collaborative working with their peers, saying that 'other children helped [them] learn' and that they also felt that 'listening to others is interesting'. They enjoyed sharing the end product with others. We produced a 'Victorian Museum' which they enjoyed sharing with parents and other classes in school. The museum consisted of a range of artefacts and presentations which the children had put together in small groups, each group having an area of Victorian life to explore in greater depth than the overview we had explored as a class in terms of more general aspects of Victorian times. This gave them plenty of opportunities for a greater degree of independence to research in books and online and enabled them to decide the best way to present their work whether it included making an artistic model, creating a presentation on the computer or a spoken or written presentation. The museum pulled each group's work together but still allowed for individuality and creativity; the children also had the opportunity to explore one area of Victorian life in depth whilst learning about the other areas from their peers. The idea of sharing across the school was not only to celebrate their work but also to share with staff the type of approach I was developing in my own class which I wanted to roll out more widely the following year. However, the joy of sharing became a regular event, and once a half term we would hold a whole school 'gallery', where we would spend a speedy twenty minutes visiting all the classrooms to see the work that had been produced. The intention was to capture the joy of sharing and for staff to share ideas and good practice.

The best endorsement of the new approach was 'Don't change anything—do the businesses next year', and a thought-provoking comment was a request for no homework! Rather than dismiss this request, it set me on a new path to explore the subject of homework which I discuss in more detail in Chapter 9.

---

**Reflection**

There are many different approaches to delivering a school curriculum, and each one has its benefits and potential drawbacks. If you are a working in a maintained school, it must incorporate the National Curriculum, but how you implement it and enhance it is still your choice. You as a school leader will need to decide on the approach or combination of approaches you wish to adopt; always remember to reflect on your school and your children. What is right for one school may not work so well for another.

The following are the core messages:

- Your school curriculum must be broad and balanced.
- Remember the freedoms you have.
- Tailor the curriculum to meet the needs of your school.
- Enjoy the craft of teaching.

---

## Bibliography

Books and articles

Vygotsky, L.S. (1978) *Mind in society: The development of higher psychological processes*, Cambridge, MA: Harvard University Press (p. 102).

## Websites

https://abcdoes.com
https://www.blackhistorymonth.org.uk
https://www.forestschoolassociation.org/what-is-forest-school
https://fieldworkeducation.com/curriculums/primary-years
https://www.focus-education.co.uk/blog/learning-challenge-curriculum-1/
https://www.mantleoftheexpert.com
https://p4c.com
https://prospectuscurriculum.co.uk
https://theblackcurriculum.com

# Chapter 9

## Homework

- How do we define *homework*?
- How does homework fit into a creative curriculum?
- What are the benefits of homework, and what are the challenges?
- Examples of one approach to homework are included.

So far we have looked at the background to curriculum and what it might look like in schools in terms of intent, implementation and impact, and I have introduced you to a few methodologies. We should now turn our attention to the topic of homework. When we were developing our curriculum, we focused on the school day and homework stayed as it was; there were reading tasks, multiplication tables and homework sheets which developed spelling, grammar or a specific maths skill. Whilst the homework was always relevant to the skills we were learning in class it didn't really fit in with the creative curriculum, it didn't follow our theme and in itself wasn't very 'creative'. It was time for that to change. Throughout this chapter, I talk through my research findings and our approaches, examining what worked well and what didn't! Much has been written about homework, and this chapter will clearly not cover all points which have been covered in a wide range of texts; however, the aim is to generate discussion and provoke further thought as well as sharing a process which I went through with one school in aligning our homework with the creative curriculum.

At the time we were developing our homework policy, there were plenty of newspaper headlines suggesting that homework was 'polluting family life' and should

DOI: 10.4324/9781003033189-9

be scrapped. A piece of research 'Homework: Learning from Practice', carried out by Penelope Weston for Ofsted in 1999 raised some key points:

- It is difficult to separate the effect of homework itself from the influence of home and family background.
- Frequency or time spent on homework is not necessarily the same thing as quality.
- A link with schoolwork, parent–school partnership and marking of work may all contribute to effective homework
- Does everyone involved have a shared understanding of what homework might look like?

Key questions which are missing here are ones of purpose: Why do we set homework, and what do we hope to achieve by it? This was our starting point. I started with a provocative question, 'Should we set our children homework?' I wanted to ascertain whether the staff felt we should and, if so, why. I had also gathered a range of views from literary research which I shared with staff after our own initial discussions and will summarise for you now.

A repeated finding which stood out for me was that the link between homework and achievement for children under the age of 11 (primary school children) was weak. If homework in primary school was not raising achievement, what was it doing? Dr Eleanor Updale (2010) argues that it is turning children into couch potatoes. It is true that homework demands can limit the time available to spend on other beneficial activities, such as sport and community involvement. She also argues that it deprives modern families of spending time together; this would have a particular impact where parents live in different homes and children spend time between the two families. Research from the Institute of Education found that homework can cause friction between children and parents leading to pressure on the child and potential educational benefits are lost. It would seem then that there are a lot of unintentional negative experiences surrounding homework. Think of your own experiences, I can certainly remember heated discussions with my mother along the lines of: 'Mrs X doesn't teach us that way and I don't understand your way'. Susan Hallam (Cowan & Hallam 1999) states that parents can confuse students by using teaching methods different from those of their teachers. Friends and family I speak to now who are parents often dread homework and are sometimes unclear of the expectations or methods used; many report the stress it generates in their households!

It seemed to me that we were looking towards abolishing homework altogether, as there is no hard evidence that in the short term, 'homework' raises educational standards in primary school, and in fact, good attendance at school, motivation and self-confidence were deemed to be the most important factors in raising achievement over and above homework. However, after much discussion, we felt that in the long term, there are many benefits which can be gained from children completing tasks set by school outside of school hours:

- Curriculum enrichment
- Willingness to learn during leisure time
- Improved attitude to school
- Better study habits and skills
- Greater self-discipline
- Better time organisation
- Developing and nurturing inquisitiveness
- More independent problem-solving
- Cooperation with others

As a staff, we distilled this list into the purpose (4 Ps) of setting homework and shared these with parents and children:

**Preparation**: To ensure readiness for the next class which might include completing activities started in class

**Participation**: To increase the involvement of students with the learning task or enjoyment of the fun of learning

**Personal Development**: To build student responsibility, perseverance, time management, self-confidence and a feeling of accomplishment; to develop and recognise students' talents in skills, possibly not taught in class; extension and enrichment

**Parent–Child Relations**: Establish communication between parent and child on the importance of schoolwork and learning; demonstrating applications of schoolwork to real-life situations and experiences, to promote parental awareness of and support of student's work and progress

I led a parent meeting during which I presented my research findings to parents and invite discussion which led in some cases to 'lively debate'. It should be remembered that homework is a highly contentious issue, in the 'Parent View' Ofsted questionnaire the question, 'My child receives appropriate homework for their age' often resulted in a 50:50 split with those who agreed and those who disagreed; however, what was never clear from this response was the various definitions of *appropriate*. This led to me design a further short survey asking parents if they felt their child received appropriate homework for their age; if not, what was it about it they felt was inappropriate – was it too much, too little – and did they like the policy of no homework in the holidays to allow for quality family time or did they prefer the flexibility of having the holidays to complete work. I also left space for any further comments. The results from this survey and the minutes of the parent meeting all contributed to our homework policy moving forwards.

Having established that homework is important and has a clear purpose within our school curriculum, we next needed to explore how much homework it was appropriate to set. We were guided by the research which suggested too much homework can lead to students losing interest in the subject or indeed learning altogether. Susan Hallam (Cowan & Hallam 1999) and the University of Durham found that those who received one piece of homework per month were more successful than those who did much more or none at all. We therefore decided to focus on quality rather than quantity of homework set, allowing time for a variety of beneficial out of school activities including quality family time. This supports the National Foundation for Educational Research findings that pupils who spend some time on a range of activities, such as reading, and extracurricular clubs perform better at school than those who limit extracurricular activities to homework alone. We worked with the findings from the University of Durham regarding monthly homework, and since a term is approximately six weeks, we explored with children and parents whether this would be a preferable option: having one piece of creative homework which lasted six weeks. Many options were offered including the weekly homework, which was at that point in operation, but the extended project appealed to many and so we trialled it for an academic year. See the examples in Boxes 9.1, 9.2 and 9.3 for Years 2, 3 and 6, respectively.

## Box 9.1 Text description of Year 2 creative project homework for parents and children to follow

### Creative Learning Log Activity Year 2

Figure 9.1: A hedgehog under vegetation. Photographer: Kalle Gustafsson, 'Hedgehog II' https://creativecommons.org/licenses/by/4.0/legalcode

**TASK OVERVIEW: *What will you discover about nocturnal animals?***

*This terms homework should link to our Creative Curriculum outlined in the Parent Overview. You will have all of term 5 to complete this homework and it should be brought to school to share with myself and the rest of Key Stage 1 for the last week of term*

*PURPOSE:*

The aim of this activity is to find out about nocturnal animals at home as well as in school. I hope you will have being more in charge of your homework. When it's all done we will look at some of the work in a special assembly and share the different ideas people have had.

(*Continued*)

*GUIDE TIME:*

We have about 5 weeks for this homework; it should take you about 2.5 hours in total. This can include about 30 minutes of thinking time and drafting. It can take longer if you are really enjoying it and want to get really creative, but it shouldn't take much less than the guide time.

*CHOICES:*

**HOW**: How will you choose to record the information? Words, pictures or a cartoon strip including both? Will you use pencil crayons, pens or paint to record what you have discovered? Will you write a short report? Could you do several drawings of the animal you have learnt about to show what you have discovered? Maybe you will use the internet to search for information and write down what you have found out? Perhaps you can visit the local or school library to look for non-fiction books that could help you? Maybe you will make a model or a sculpture of a nocturnal animal? Maybe could take photographs of you working hard and stick them into your creative Learning Log?
It is up to you!

**WHO**: You may choose who you work with. Your family might like to help you, or you may choose to work alone. Just make sure you write all the names of the people who helped you with your work.

*PRESENTATION:*

The way you present the work is up to you, but try to keep a record in your learning log to help you remember what you found out.

*CHALLENGE:*

Will you research more than one nocturnal animal?
Could you visit a wildlife sanctuary with your family and take some photos?
Could you use the information you have discovered to make your garden a safer place for wild animals and birds?

**Box 9.2   Text description of Year 3 creative project**
**homework for parents and children to follow**

**Creative Learning Log Activity Year 3**

Figure 9.2: A Mexican Flag. Nicolas Raymond, 'Mexico Grunge Flag' https://creativecommons.
org/licenses/by/4.0/legalcode

*TASK OVERVIEW: What will you discover about Mexico?*

*This terms homework links to our Creative Curriculum outlined in the Parent Overview. You will have all of term 5 to complete this homework, and it should be brought to school to share with myself and the rest of Key Stage 2 in the last week of term.*

*PURPOSE:*

The aim of this activity is to find out about Mexico at home as well as in school. I hope you will have fun being more in charge of your homework. When it's all done we will look at some of the work in a special assembly and share what we have discovered

*(Continued)*

*GUIDE TIME:*

We have about 5 weeks for this homework, and it should take you about 2.5 hours in total. This can include about 30 minutes of thinking time and drafting. It can take longer if you are really enjoying it, but it shouldn't take much less than the guide time.

*CHOICES:*

**HOW**: How will you choose to record the information? Words, pictures or a cartoon strip including both? Will you use pencil crayons, pens or paint to record what you have discovered? Will you write a short report? Could you do several drawings of different aspects you have learnt about to show what you have discovered? Maybe you will use the internet to search for information and write down what you have found out? Perhaps you can visit the local or school library to look for books that could help you? Maybe you will make a model or a sculpture of something you have found out about? Maybe could take photographs of you working hard and stick them into your creative Learning Log? Maybe you will ask someone at home to help you with some Mexican cooking? It is up to you!

**WHO**: You may choose who you work with. Your family might like to help you or you may choose to work alone. Just make sure you write all the names of the people who helped you with your work.

*PRESENTATION:*

The way you present the work is up to you, but try to keep a record in your learning log to help you remember what you found out.

*CHALLENGE:*

What **four** aspects of Mexico will you research in your mini project?

A landmark?
A person?
A food?
Clothes?
A city?

These are just some ideas you may add your own if you wish.

**Box 9.3    Text description of Year 6 creative project
homework for parents and children to follow**

### Year 6 Revision Homework

Figure 9.3: A pair of spectacles and a pen sat on top of a document which has been partly highlighted. https://creativecommons.org/licenses/by/4.0/legalcode

*TASK OVERVIEW: What will your revision 'tool' look like?*

*To help with revision of areas of maths, everyone in Year 6 will have the change to create something fun to help each other improve a 'wobbly' area of maths. It should be fun and something we can enjoy using or watching in the week before SATs [Standard Attainment Tests], which is why it is due in on 8 May.*

*USEFUL INFORMATION:*

Your 'revision tool' must help a Year 6 child to improve their maths skills.

(*Continued*)

*PURPOSE:*

The aim of this activity is to **find a fun way to revise and improve your maths skills!** It is a good idea to choose an area you are 'wobbly' on so that you can use this homework to keep practicing and get it right. Maybe you easily forget 2D shape names or some of your tables facts?

*GUIDE TIME:*

As we have about 3 weeks for this homework it should take you about 3 hours, this can include about 30 minutes of thinking time and drafting. It can take longer if you are really enjoying it and want to get really creative but it shouldn't take much less than the guide time.

*CHOICES:*

**WHAT**: What will your 'tool' be, a game show recorded on your webcam? A board game to play on rainy days? A booklet to practice and improve? A game to play on the computer? Perhaps you can think of something else; it is up to you! Just make sure you include some notes/planning and perhaps a finished photo or your favourite still image from your game show taken from the webcam in your Learning Log.

**WHO**: You may choose who you work with or you may choose to work alone; include all the names of the contributors to your work.

*PRESENTATION:*

The way you present the work is up to you, please see the ideas above. Remember to include

- Instructions if it is a game
- A funky container for your DVD or game or an eye-catching cover for your booklet
- An explanation of how your product will help children improve their maths
- Counters/dice or anything else you think it needs

*CHALLENGE:*

How can you be sure Year 6 children will WANT to play it/watch it/use it? Will you have more than one area of maths or keep it simple and do it well? How will your product be different to any others?

Each year group had their own focus linked to class learning, but the homework overview looked very similar for each year group identifying the task overview, useful information, purpose, guide time (as requested by parents at the meeting), choices open to the learners and information on the expectations about how it was to be presented or again the freedoms open to them. We also included challenges for those who felt the homework was too simplistic and wished to stretch themselves further.

This homework seemed to work very well in terms of pupil outcomes and staff workload. We celebrated the work termly; visiting classrooms for 'homework galleries' where impressive models of Roman longships or Egyptian pyramids would be displayed or revision games, masks or home movies on a topic the children had learned about in school. Little written feedback was received from parents, although it was obvious some outcomes had more parental input than others.

At the next parent meeting, however, during which we reviewed the changes, there was a lot of negative feedback from parents who felt that they were having to guide their child's learning and teachers had pushed responsibility on to them. They felt disconnected with the classroom learning in general (which was the opposite of our intentions), and their knowledge of what was being taught in class was limited to the focus for the piece of homework. Many who had previously wanted the extended homework now felt it was too long. It was time for us to rethink!

From these discussions and further research, in order to reconnect parents to the curriculum, we regularly produced parent curriculum overviews (Figures 9.4–9.6).

The intention for this was that parents were aware of the subjects we were covering in a particular topic, and homework was changed significantly in that we offered a range of smaller tasks over a shorter period. We allowed a fortnight on average for homework to be completed rather than six weeks so that we maintained our stance on valuing family time and out-of-school activities, and it did not revert to the pressure felt by many of weekly homework. This reviewed approach allowed for flexibility of busy lifestyles and parents living apart but gave more guidance to parents and more structure for the children within a shorter time frame. This involved more research and discussion with other schools to explore a range of options, then with our staff to make it our own and with parents and children to share the new format which also included a space for fortnightly feedback from parents, grandparents or children themselves.

This was quite a change from the more open-ended longer-term creative projects and rather than a particular creative output we incorporated creative thinking and

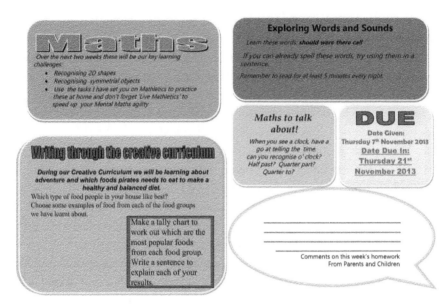

Figure 9.4: An example of Year 2 homework

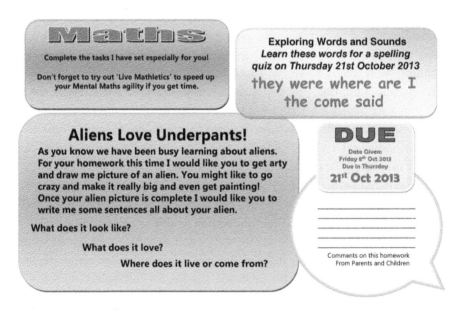

Figure 9.5: An example of Year 1 homework

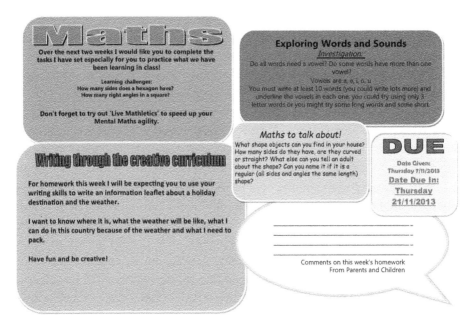

Figure 9.6: An example of Year 3 homework

the application of skills which had been taught in class. The purpose of 'Mathletics' which was our chosen platform at the time, was to focus on fluency, to ensure pupils had opportunities to practice the skills they had been taught in class. It also enabled us to track progress and identify additional needs through the assessment data which the programme collected. We had to be wary of pupils having additional support by parents so the higher scores were not as reliable an indicator of success as the lower scores were of requiring additional support, however many of our more able pupils enjoyed the challenges presented to them and were regular visitors to the site, choosing to complete their own challenges as well as those set for homework! For those who did not have access to a computer/internet at home, I ran a weekly Mathletics club which also served as a catch-up 'club' for those who were regularly missing homework despite having access to the equipment at home. The purpose of 'Literacy through the Creative Curriculum' was to apply the skills we had taught in literacy (later renamed English) in the context of our wider theme for the term. This also shared with parents the skills we were learning as well as the theme which would illustrate the outline we shared on the Parent Overview document. I used to open up opportunities here for creative output and suggest that the child could produce a poster, slideshow, brochure or write a script for a TV or radio show and present it if they so wished. Therefore, there was an option but not an expectation of creative output, if it suited the child, and they had those facilities available to them such as a parent's mobile phone to record on or a computer with a presentation programme they could be as creative as they wished. If it was a busy family weekend or there was limited access to resources, it was still possible to complete the same homework task in a different way. The purpose of 'Maths to Talk About' was to generate discussion around the dinner table, on a walk or in the car for example. The idea was to make it easy to slot into daily life and not be too onerous; it was an optional piece of work as it was tricky to monitor and the core purpose here was to keep parents informed of some of the knowledge and skills their child had been learning recently so that they could continue to talk about it beyond the homework deadline. Some children chose to write notes about their discussion, others didn't, and I'm sure there were some who may have chosen not to complete it at all, but it was a communication tool for parents and a reminder for the children about what we had been learning in class. Spelling almost warrants its own chapter! I am not a fan of learning lists of words as I feel this is akin to cramming for tests which I refer to in this book. I would encourage children to identify spelling patterns and to create 'silly sentences' with their words in order to try to help them retain them, and we would test the children weekly. It was easy to administer and gave an almost instant measure of success, but my concern is that of retention. Learning spelling strategies and understanding the meaning of words are much more beneficial to pupils gaining a long-term skill of spelling. However, some parents seem to like the idea of a spelling list as do some school leaders, and at this point, it was our chosen approach.

Engaging with stakeholders and listening carefully to learners and parents especially was crucial to the journey we were on with homework. I led assemblies where I asked children to share their views and invited class teachers to lead discussions in their own classes, feeding back their findings. For parents I provided emailed and paper copies of surveys and invited parents to attend presentation meetings during which I shared my research and listened to their views. Whilst I knew I wasn't going to please everyone given the 50:50 split I mentioned earlier, I not only upheld the values of the 4 Ps when making any decision but also wove into this the practical considerations to meet the needs of learners and parents. Annual reviews kept us on track and ensured continued progress in this area with small adjustments here and there. The result was better engagement with homework, greater connection between home and school and an increase in creative thinking such as making connections and solving problems. Homework could also lead to some impressive creative outputs from time to time. Children were encouraged to choose how to present their work, which allowed for creative output too, perhaps creating a short film, cooking, creating a song or a presentation, a cartoon strip or creating a game. The emphasis, however, was on creative thinking so as not to disadvantage children to did not have access to digital devices, building materials or wider skills and support in their extended families, and there was no expectation for example that children would build their own impressive Viking longships from recycled materials or matchsticks with a grandparent, although many chose to do just this. Please see Box 9.4 which addresses some 'frequently asked questions' from parents regarding homework, which highlights this point about creative output amongst others.

---

**Box 9.4  Frequently asked questions about homework by parents**

**Frequently Asked Questions**

Q  How will we ensure that children are fully engaged and do not leave the work until the last minute?

A  This is down to dialogue between children, teachers and parents. Every homework will be set using the same-style information sheet; this is for parents and children. In Key Stage 1 if you are unsure of what is required it may be helpful for parents to check the sheet and if it is still unclear then check with the teacher, from Key Stage 2 this should be the child's responsibility.

Q  How is the school going to ensure that the creative homework draws in key curriculum skills?

A  These areas will be identified on the homework planning sheets. Each homework will draw on skills within a range of subjects, but not every subject will be utilised every time. Throughout the year there will be a spread of subject areas.

Q  How can parents to feedback during the next stage of the journey?

A  We invite you and your child to comment on the homework in the learning logs, what they particularly enjoyed, what new learning took place and any challenges they faced.

*(Continued)*

---

> Q What about Year 6 with secondary school transition?
> A With regard to secondary school, the emphasis is on 'independent study' and the ability to read and research and to analyse, enquire, innovate and evaluate. It is these 'higher-order' thinking skills and study habits we are aiming to foster.
>
> Q 'I don't have internet access or resources at home'; does that matter?
> A The homework is about creative interpretation of the task, more about creative THINKING than making. A drawing or a piece of writing creatively done can be just as effective as a model or a role-play recorded on a webcam.

This was our journey with homework at the time. Just as the curriculum is unique to the school, so is the approach to homework. In other schools I had links with, this creative 'extended project' approach had worked very well, so it very much depends on your school, but for us, it was not well received by the majority at that time. It perhaps needs to be tested before you know how effective it is going to be, but I hope that the insights into our journey and the feedback from our parents provides some food for thought.

> - Why do we set homework; what do we hope to achieve by it?
> - If we are going to continue setting homework, how frequently will it be set?
> - What will homework look like?
> - What do we need to consider regarding equality of opportunity? (One example to consider is access to the internet.)
> - Will it be difficult for any of our students to complete the homework, and how can we mitigate against this?

## Bibliography

### Books and articles

Cowan, R. & Hallam, S. (1999) *What do we know about homework?* London: Institute of Education, University of London.

Updale, E. (2010) *Homework? A total waste of time* TES Online Available from: https://www.tes.com/news/homework-total-waste-time Accessed 6 November 2019.

Weston, P. (1999) *Homework Learning from Practice*, London: The Stationery Office.

# Chapter 10

## Curriculum provision during a pandemic

- What does intent, implementation and impact look like during a pandemic?
- How has the pandemic affected creativity?
- How has it changed our delivery of the curriculum?
- What will the impact of the pandemic be on returning to face-to-face learning in the classroom for all children?

At the time of writing this book, we are amid a pandemic. COVID-19 is caused by a novel coronavirus disease, first identified in December 2019 in China. The World Health Organization (WHO) declared the outbreak of COVID-19 a pandemic on 11 March 2020. The WHO stated that 'most people infected will experience mild to moderate respiratory illness and will recover without special treatment'. However, for some people, this illness will be very serious, requiring ventilation and for some fatal; in fact, the daily death toll has been over 1,000 (within 28 days of a positive COVID-19 test), and the total number of deaths to date is over 100,000. I'm sorry to have to talk such doom and gloom in a book about education, creativity and curriculum, but it is important for this chapter (especially for those of you reading this much later than 2020/2021) to set the context. I have been amazed, however, by the creativity which has been borne out of such dark times; for example a vacuum cleaner company is one of the companies that has turned themselves to designing ventilation systems, small gin distilleries have produced alcohol sanitiser gel for use on hands rather than drinking alcohol and individuals in their own homes have sewn 'scrub' tops and trousers for nurses and doctors due to the rapid turnaround required and limited kits available. There are many more companies and individuals creating screens for use in hairdressers and reception areas and those who have

DOI: 10.4324/9781003033189-10

creatively adapted shower screens or such like for this purpose. These examples merely scratch the surface of the emerging creativity we have been witness to.

The original strain of the virus was said to be easily transmissible, and there have since been variants that are claimed to be up to 80% more transmissible than the original. Due to this and to there being no vaccine available for COVID-19 initially, in the UK we have experienced three 'lockdowns', with tight limits on our social freedoms, only going out for essential shopping, medical needs or limited exercise with members of your own household. During the first (March 2020) and third lockdown (January 2021), schools were closed to most pupils except those of vulnerable children and children of key workers, and remote learning in schools was commonplace. It is this remote learning which I focus on in this chapter through the lenses of intent, implementation and impact.

## Intent

The intent has been embedded in the context of each lockdown; the first in March 2020 was originally perceived by many of us to be for a couple of weeks in the lead-up to the spring break followed by this two-week holiday and then a return to school, so the intent (for the school I was working in at the time) was to use these two weeks to recap previously taught lessons. People were being asked by the prime minister to 'work from home if you can', and some families were isolating at home due to having symptoms of the virus, believing they may have been in contact with someone who may have had the virus or, in my view, they were extremely nervous. Due to this many schools, including my own, attended emergency staff meetings to learn how to use an online platform for learning and in the same week the prime minister announced that schools were to close. With approximately 50% of children in attendance the following day, we prepared children for remote learning as best we could ensuring they knew how to log into the platform and had an exercise book to record work in if they preferred to work on paper or were without a printer or computer access. It should be remembered that at this point, few, if any, of us had taught online before, so whilst it was exciting and challenged our creativity, it was at times pretty daunting.

It soon became clear that the lockdown was going to last longer than two weeks and it was not enough to just recap previously taught lessons, so we all had to think about our intent and how this had now changed. We needed to utilise the learning platform to deliver the curriculum that we would have been delivering in school but do this online for the majority of pupils. This was replicated in many schools in various ways. To make the experience as equitable as we possibly could, we planned the online work for all children whether at school or at home, and if the children were at school, they did have teacher support and school laptops available to complete the core work in the mornings with physical education and craft activities in the afternoons. Whilst our intent was to deliver the curriculum as similarly as we could in school, there were a number of disparities between families: the amount of adult help available, access to a digital device, access to a printer or the ability to afford ink and paper especially for people who were on reduced salaries due to furlough, or even access to craft-type resources for more practical activities which we would have in school. Our intent therefore encompassed the need to be aware of all these differences and to ensure that all activities could be carried out in a number of ways, access to resources or not and 'remotely', not just 'online', in school or at home. We were also aware of children's mental health during this challenging time, with lots of information in the media, parental stress and illness or death of family members, so we wanted to keep children learning, keep connecting with them and support them as best we could without being in the same room as each other. Our intent for the curriculum was clear; however, the challenge was in implementing the intended plan bearing in mind some of the key issues I have already raised.

## Implementation

As I alluded to earlier, this was the most challenging aspect of remote learning. Practitioners were all learning a new skill in teaching remotely whether that was via the internet or packs of learning sent home on paper. At the same time as applying that learning to delivering high-quality lessons for our students. There was a need to keep incredibly open minds and personalise learning to as many different scenarios as possible. Having explored provision in a range of schools (through speaking with friends who are parents, others who are teachers and, of course, some who are both), the platform being used to deliver the learning played a large part in our methodology. For some who had access to livestreaming option, there was a closer similarity to classroom teaching, although class discussions are much easier in person than online as anyone who has attended an online meeting will attest to! In my case, we did not have this function available so we would set work with either an online resource to explain the task or a paper copy of a slideshow for example. Occasionally I would also pre-record a short explanation, although given my terribly slow broadband speed and the length of time it took me to upload, these were few and far between. There would then be a selection of work at three different 'challenge levels' for the children to choose from in maths and English, in particular, or an open-ended task for many of the other subjects with a range of options for the children to select and complete making sure that every child could complete at least one of them with very limited equipment. We also had to ensure that the same learning task was available to those children who did not have access to a computer and who therefore needed work in hard copy format.

Motivating children to work and setting the learning environment, such as a quiet and conducive space, were out of our hands for those children who were learning at home. This is where the parent involvement is key, and many parents are also working from home or have more than one child at home, most likely at different ages, working at different levels perhaps at different schools all setting work and various platforms. The struggles parents have been through in encouraging their children to complete schoolwork and supporting them with subjects adults may be unfamiliar with have been shared on social media. On their return to school, some children have reported that they enjoyed being at home, finding that working alone has meant fewer distractions and that they have been able to complete tasks more efficiently than when in class. However, others have really struggled to understand concepts with a lack of support or limited motivation. Some parents have wanted more work for their child whilst others said the amount being set is more than they would usually do in a school day which is broken up by playtime with friends and lunchtime socialising, which, of course, were missing for so many children. It is my contention that learning in this way is more intense, that we are all (children, parents and teachers) at the time of writing mentally strained with the uncertainty of what we are living through and that whilst it is very important to continue to provide learning opportunities for our children, it is important to remember all the challenges I have outlined and the difference between collaborative learning in class and learning in isolation (especially for those without live video links and a means to communicate with the teacher at the point of explanation). We made ourselves available to the children throughout the day so that we could answer questions, but this was in the form of written responses to emails which could be sent by children or parents any time of day or night, which would lead to an inbox full of emails awaiting a response. This is a very different experience of feedback compared to live teaching! It is for this reason, in my view, that we should perhaps temporarily streamline the curriculum (which goes against everything I have said in previous chapters and goes against everything I believe under normal circumstances) and build even stronger links to cross-curricular themes so that we can continue to educate our children, combining subject skills from one area and knowledge from another without overwhelming them. One school I have spoken to focuses on 'Book Talk', which encompasses reading for decoding and comprehension, and then core lessons of English and maths. The topics are in the form of 'quests' which children can select from; one example of a task within a quest is to build a Sikh temple.

Another test which presented itself during 'lockdown teaching' was monitoring engagement. For those who were working online, it was a simple task to track who had made contact to ask questions and who had handed in the assignments which had been set. The greater challenge was tracking those who were working on assignments at home which had either been set by the school or for those who were choosing to follow their own 'smorgasbord' of activities available. These activities were offered by well-meaning celebrities who found themselves temporarily out of work and wanting to help within their specialist area or by the BBC through its BBC Bitesize activities which have always been available but were now being heavily promoted to parents to pick and choose from. Children in most schools were not encouraged to bring in hard copies of their work on a regular basis due to risks of infection which were thought to have been increased and would have encouraged traffic to the school gates at a time when national restrictions were in force. This has huge implications for monitoring engagement and levels of participation; in fact, one child, on returning to school, claimed he had not completed any learning in lockdown despite the school providing a laptop for learning (the family has Wi-Fi) and paper copies prior to the laptop loan. His mother corroborated this assertion and said that due to home circumstances and other younger children in the household, it made it very challenging for her to support his learning. I am sure there will be others in a similar situation, but I hope these children are in the minority as school staff have worked very hard during this period to ensure all children have access to learning.

Homeschooling is, of course, an option for any parent as stated in Section 7 of the Education Act 1996:

> The parent of every child of compulsory school age shall cause him to receive efficient full-time education suitable – (a) to his age, ability and aptitude, and (b) to any special educational needs he may have, either by regular attendance at school or otherwise.
>
> (UK Parliament 1996)

There are benefits to homeschooling, such as very personalised learning and individualised support, and drawbacks, for example the limited social interaction and perhaps parental confidence in delivering some areas of the curriculum. It is certainly a decision not taken lightly but carefully considered; however, this is not one of those situations. No one is expected to 'home educate' their child for the long haul, and this type of home learning situation is not all on the parent. The planning and delivery of lessons (on paper, via video or through narrated presentations) are carried out by the teacher. The parent is often in the same physical space as the child whereas for many the teacher is not; the parent's role is therefore more one of support, encouragement and providing the space in which the child can learn. We are (or, at least, we should be) working in tandem to meet the learning needs of our children under challenging circumstances.

One unique difficulty, however, can arise when a parent has not officially opted to home educate their child, the child is still registered at the school and the school is responsible for delivering the curriculum, but the parent chooses to create their own 'mix and match' curriculum from the wide range of rich resources available for a time and at some point in the near future the child will return to school with the school accountable for their progress. Inevitably, there will be gaps in the school's intent and what has been implemented. This leads on to the next focus: 'impact'.

## Curriculum impact

Let us remind ourselves of the quote I used from Ofsted earlier in this book which I shall paraphrase: Impact can be measured by pupils knowing and being able to do more. It is important then that once we regain a type of normality, we assess, in age-appropriate ways, what it is that the students know and can do. This assessment should be used to inform the teachers of the gaps in learning for each individual so that we can support these children to be ready for the next steps in their learning.

Ofsted carried out more than 900 visits to education and social care providers during September and October 2020 to hear how providers are coping with the challenges of a new academic year amidst a pandemic. A key finding has been that children with special educational needs and those with disabilities have been particularly affected due to the additional services that families relied on, such as speech and language or physiotherapy, being largely unavailable. Some providers have been innovative in their approach for example supporting parents via online platforms to carry out physiotherapy by modelling exercises with a doll for parents to replicate at home; however, this would seem to be a rarity rather than the norm.

An additional concerning impact of school closures is that referrals to social care teams have fallen. This may be perceived as a positive trend and could indicate that situations at home have rapidly improved during the lockdowns, with children being safer than before; however, it could also be that children were out of sight from school staff who might normally notice behaviours or injuries, causing concern and following this up with a referral, so it is plausible to be concerned that abuse, exploitation or neglect is going undetected.

What we have to remember is that there has been a disruption to education all over the world. In the UK, children will have missed gaps in two academic years: during the first lockdown in March 2020, and then on returning to their new class in September, they had some sense of normality until Christmas. After a period of face-to-face learning and the start of 'catch-up learning' for those identified children who were most affected by the first lockdown, there was a further lockdown with primary schools being closed on 5 January 2021 and returning on 8 March 2021. The full educational impact is yet to be seen and will likely play out for many years to come; this should be taken into account in terms of accountability measures and support. However, this will have to be planned carefully so that children have the stepping-stones to move forward with their learning but are not missing the new learning because of the interventions in place to plug their gaps! This will have to be carefully thought out and integrated into daily lesson planning, perhaps, as is currently the case, informally assessing the level of understanding to identify the starting point for groups of children and knowing who to support and who to challenge. In tandem with this is the need to support children's mental well-being and, in particular, those children who in normal times may have been referred to social services for support but have missed out due to the limitations of lockdown as well as those with Special Educational Needs and Disabilities who may need intensive support to catch up on their additional needs. I have no doubt that teachers will continue to support pupil's learning, and I am not suggesting account-ability should be scrapped. What I am saying is that we as practitioners and those who hold schools to account have to be aware of the impact a pandemic has on a child's life experiences, learning opportunities and challenges, as well as, importantly, their mental and physical well-being.

---

- How has COVID-19 affected the children in your school, physically, mentally, emotionally and academically?
- How do you know where the gaps in academic learning are?
- What are you doing to try to close these gaps?

---

## Bibliography

### Journals and reports

Parliament of the United Kingdom (1996) *Education Act 1996*, London: The Stationery Office Available from: https://www.legislation.gov.uk/ukpga/1996/56/section/7/enacted Accessed 5 January 2020.

Ofsted (2020) *Children hardest hit by COVID-19 pandemic are regressing in basic skills and learning* Available from: https://www.gov.uk/government/news/ofsted-children-hardest-hit-by-covid-19-pandemic-are-regressing-in-basic-skills-and-learning Accessed 5 January 2020.

### Websites

https://www.who.int/health-topics/coronavirus Accessed 3 February 2020.

# Chapter 11

## Conclusion

- What have we discussed in this book?
- What is critical for the future of education?
- What will you 'take away' from reading this book; how will it impact your practice?

In summary, we have defined *curriculum* and looked at the context society plays in shaping this and how it has changed over time. We have analysed the need for a broad and balanced curriculum against the limitations of cramming for success and delved into the process of curriculum planning, delivery and evaluation using Ofsted's terminology. I have shared some examples of lessons and a range of different approaches you may wish to explore. We raised questions about homework and discussed the challenges all educators faced in 2020/2021 when we were plunged into a pandemic. To aid your reflection, I outline in a little more detail each of the areas we have looked at. Use the reflective questions at the end of each chapter to understand what this means for you and your setting. Perhaps you are reading this alone as a school leader or a classroom practitioner, or maybe you are leading curriculum development staff training and you could use these questions as a stimulus for discussion with your staff.

We started by identifying that the National Curriculum and Early Years Foundation Stage Framework are only parts of the whole-school curriculum and that broad and balanced creative experiences including visits and visitors to our schools complement the educational diet for our children. We understand that providing opportunities for children to think creatively helps them in the here

DOI: 10.4324/9781003033189-11

and now and prepares them for the future, applying knowledge and skills across the curriculum to solve new problems they may be faced with. Understanding the freedoms and legal obligations of our roles gives us licence to be more creative in our teaching, feeling less restricted and robotic, and re-ignites the passion for the craft of teaching. Key turning points in history helped us understand a bit more about the nature and purpose of the school curriculum as well as how this has changed over time. The school curriculum should prepare children for their future, both in the workplace and in social situations; they should able to debate, discuss and listen to others and confidently formulate their own views. A narrowed curriculum came about for a variety of reasons but due, in part, to an early prescriptive national curriculum, leaving little room for interpretation. The pressure of exam results and achievement data showing targets being hit also contributed to the narrowing of the curriculum to focus on the areas that would be tested and easily measured. This was regardless of the quality of learning experienced by the person behind the data. This prompted the question of 'intent' in a school curriculum: What is it that we want children to know and be able to do at which stage in their development?

In Chapter 3, we delved a little deeper into what is meant by 'creativity' and the ambiguity of definitions amongst practitioners and researchers. We focused our attention on creative thinking and why this is important for the economy and the individual. The teacher's role in developing creative thinking was discussed and how this is a cultural shift for many. 'Carte blanche' creates its own unique challenges and is balanced against the National Curriculum base, setting out the minimum educational expectation for every child, within a framework of freedom which allows each establishment to be creative and tailor the curriculum to the needs of the children in their setting. Each subject in turn was looked at, explaining the skills and knowledge we gain from each as well as highlighting the opportunities for creative thought. We looked at proposals for a new curriculum which never fully took flight but has left seeds of creativity behind, with many schools making their own links between subjects and providing opportunities for children to apply their skills in different circumstances to the ones in which they were taught. I used a piece of high-quality text to illustrate how essential it is that we teach children a wide range of subjects and topic areas within the subjects to support their comprehension of reading and their ability to make connections in learning and in life itself. Wider experiences such as outdoor learning, adventurous activity weeks, drama, Forest School and open-ended investigations at all ages are crucial if we are to provide children with rich learning experiences providing them with useful life skills. The Early Years has a lot to offer, in particular the recognition of 'characteristics for effective learning', which should not be confined to the Early Years of children's education.

- Is the learner engaged? Are they keen to 'have a go'? Do they play around with what they know, and do they like to find things out for themselves? Identified in Early Years as 'Playing and Exploring'.
- How motivated and resilient are they? Are they able to concentrate, and do they enjoy and learn with purpose? Labelled in Early Years as 'Active Learning'.
- Do they have original ideas, make links and choose methods, Otherwise called 'Creating and Thinking Critically'?

These elements should form the core of compulsory education from 0 to 18. Each strand will look different for each age range and indeed for each pupil according to their needs, but they are applicable to all learners and should be at the heart of all learning.

In Chapter 5, we looked at 'curriculum champions', the role of senior leaders in coordinating and overseeing curriculum development as well as the individual roles of subject leaders combining leadership and management, managing a curriculum budget to ensure efficiency and effectiveness, promoting their subject across the school and supporting teachers' pedagogy and subject knowledge to maintain high-quality teaching and learning. We then turned our attention to children are unique individuals but acknowledging that they also fit into a number of 'groups' in terms of learning. Many of these groups have specific challenges which need to be overcome so that there are no barriers for a child to reach their potential. The role of the creative curriculum in addressing some of these challenges was also studied. Ofsted's terminology of 'intent, implementation and impact' was explored, understanding that the curriculum goes through the process of being designed, delivered and measured for effectiveness. In this chapter, I shared my insights having been on the journey of developing a school curriculum in the hope that some of this learning will support you on your journey, and I also offer some examples of teaching and learning from myself and colleagues, highlighting the benefits of each particular activity linking learning not only to the National Curriculum objectives but also more broadly to a variety of other aspects of learning such as enrichment, well-being and personal development for the learner.

In Chapter 8 I shared different approaches to delivering a school curriculum and each one has its benefits and potential drawbacks. The golden rule with any approach is to reflect upon your school and your children; what is right for one school may not work so well for another. This is so true also for excellent learning in one country that works well and has positive benefits to the children and wider community. Some elements may work, the entire approach may work or indeed none of it at all due to the fact that a school curriculum is bound up in the culture of the country of origin. I felt this very strongly when visiting Finland and learning about some of their practices which worked well but understanding that they were wrapped up in the culture and the priorities of the country at any one time in history, an important consideration. I remind you to ensure that your school curriculum must be broad and balanced, to remember the freedoms you have ensure you are meeting the needs of your school and to enjoy the craft of teaching. We explored how homework fits into the creative curriculum, looking at the benefits and challenges. Again I shared my personal journey, the processes and pitfalls we encountered as a school. It is a useful point at which to pause, reflect and ask if there is a need for homework at all and justify your reasoning behind it. In this chapter I shared examples of how homework looked at different stages of the journey and why we adapted our approach over time.

At the time of writing, we are in the midst of the COVID-19 pandemic, and it would seem remiss of me not to include a reflection on this in relation to the school curriculum. We look more deeply at the effect a pandemic has had on the curriculum in the UK, in particular the lockdowns and partial school closures, the move to online learning and the restrictions some children are facing due to difficulties accessing a digital device. We also explored the smorgasbord of opportunities available and the excitement of famous faces delivering rich content coupled with the 'pick 'n' mix' approach by some parents, leading to a wide variety of experiences children will have had when they return to school several months later.

In the future, it will be important that we continue to develop critical and creative thinkers who will be able to solve unique problems which they might come across in their future and to take on jobs which may not yet have been invented by applying skills and knowledge they have been given access to through their education. The pandemic has further highlighted the need to ensure we prioritise mental health and wellbeing providing strategies for coping when life gets tough. This will help young people not only learn more effectively but also enjoy life more fully and to reduce the financial impact on the National Health Service later in life as there should be fewer crisis calls if a range of approaches are already in place. At the extreme end of this, educating children about mental well-being and healthy choices could even save lives; it really is that important. This should not solely be down to individual schools but, in fact, should also be a national priority led by our government. Personal, Social, Health and Economic education as a whole, not just relationships education, although this is a good start, needs a higher profile and should be part of any revised national curriculum.

Assessment measures the impact of any teaching and learning and should certainly be the at the end and not the beginning of the learning cycle; by that I mean that we should not 'teach to the test' we should value and promote a rich, well-rounded curriculum with a balance of all subjects and a breadth of different topic areas and experiences. Assessment, such as formative assessment, will help us measure progress along the way and identify misconceptions or gaps in understanding, and summative assessment should measure what has been taught, not determine the curriculum which is to be taught as has unfortunately been the case in many schools in recent years. Ofsted has acknowledged its focus on data has fed this development, so hopefully now, with a shift to the quality of education that children are receiving in terms of intent, implementation and impact, schools will feel empowered to do what is right for their children and focus on the educational diet on offer. A child has one chance at their education; let us make it outstanding for all of them.

The aim of this book is to give practitioners like you, the confidence to understand your freedoms and your legal obligations so that you can celebrate the successes of your own exciting and engaging creative curriculum, as well as to provide insights which challenge you to reflect. I hope that I have achieved that.

---

- What are your legal obligations? How do you ensure you fulfil them?
- What are your freedoms and how do you make use of them?
- What are you proud of that your school do well?
- What will you take from this book and apply in your school?

---

# Index

Page numbers in **Bold** indicate tables, page numbers in *Italics* indicate figures.